ZANSKAR

Photographs by Olivier Föllmi · Text by Jacques Poget · *With 102 colour photographs*

Thames and Hudson

ZANSKAR

A Himalayan Kingdom

My thanks to Serge Fouillet for his great friendship
O.F.

Translated from the French by Ruth Sharman

First published in Great Britain in 1989
by Thames and Hudson Ltd, London

© 1988 Éditions Nathan (Paris – France)

All Rights Reserved. No part of this publication may be reproduced or transmitted in any form or by any means, electronic or mechanical, including photocopy, recording or any other information storage and retrieval system, without prior permission in writing from the publisher.

Printed in Switzerland

A KINGDOM IN THE SKY

Zang-skar: gentle plosion, soft release of sound; in ancient Tibetan the name denotes a river and three valleys situated in a remote corner of the world. A tiny kingdom long known only to the few: inaccessible, unyielding, and therefore forgotten. Entrenched behind passes over 16,000 feet high and which are closed from November to June, the region's eight thousand inhabitants live on barley and tea made with salted yak butter.

Zanskar nestles between its mountains like a hanging garden: a winter garden and a summer garden. It has only two seasons, beautiful and brutal in their extremes, and life there is arduous, but, as yet, natural and tranquil. It is a garden of the past, scarcely touched by the nineteenth century, not yet ravaged by the twentieth.

Refuge of a simple form of Tibetan Buddhism, witness still to a style of life that is fast disappearing, Zanskar perches at the northern tip of India, between the River Indus and the chain of the Great Himalaya. The River Zanskar flows into the Indus, forming a link with neighbouring Ladakh.

Leaning up against the small roofless stone wall which serves as a shelter to travellers, we listen to the roaring of the river below us. We are hemmed in by four huge rocky peaks, up whose smooth, steep sides the path threads with difficulty. Beside the wall a small ochre-coloured *chörten*, a shrine to Buddha, courageously proclaims the presence of man – and of God – in this mineral world where darkness descends so suddenly.

It is exactly a quarter of an hour since Nawang Tomtches and Tzering Norges set down their load fastened to a wood and rope frame and collected a few twigs here and there, some donkey and horse droppings and ten cakes of yak dung. The water is singing in the cooking pot which straddles three stones; Norges breaks off a piece of dung, tests its dryness with his thumb and slips it delicately into the embers. While the tea is drawing, he takes a pouch of barley flour out of his bag and kneads it into dough.

The procedure and the equipment are the same whether they are in their own kitchen or camping out in the open. With such simple conditions still governing their daily lives, these people are born campers. They live as their ancestors lived: autonomous, self-sufficient, needing nothing and nobody in order to survive in these inhospitable mountains. It's their world, which they wouldn't change . . . for anything in the world.

Although they are peasants not porters by trade, they know all the paths; their family has long maintained the tradition of the caravan, though conducted tourist parties are beginning to take its place today.

We eat in silence and drink the tea. Norges feeds the fire sparingly, just keeping it aglow. Tomtches pulls out a ball of yak wool from the depths of his *goncha* (a thick woollen robe) and spins it between his thumb and index finger. With his penknife he cuts a section from the flap of the garment, takes a needle from his hat and quietly sews the material over the gaping hole in his rubber shoe. The sky is swarming with stars. More than anywhere else? The rocky peaks which stand sentinel round the camp seem to bite into a Milky Way that is astonishingly close and bright. Zanskar is a kingdom in the sky.

It is the kingdom of light, a light that is ever-changing, deploying its many splendours over a sheer and empty landscape which it endlessly re-creates. The mountains rise to 20,000 feet of scorched earth and compressed, tortured rock. They burst in a jagged line towards the sky, pierce the clouds, a colourful multi-layered testimony to recent great geological upheavals – of less than fifty million years ago. The Himalayas are young in terms of the earth as a whole; that is why they are dominated by vertical lines. Everything – peaks, gorges, valleys, distances, even shadows – is immeasurable here, a gateway to infinity. The silence itself has a peculiar density. This vastness, though threatening at times, evokes a feeling of profound serenity. Zanskar is a peaceful land where everything, even drama, seems natural, part of the order of things.

Tomtches and Norges wrap themselves in their blankets and drop off to sleep, just as if they were at home, in Pishu, the last village on the plain. They are father and son, fifty-five and twenty-eight years of age, and members of a large family. Memele ('grandfather') Sadup Targes, the oldest inhabitant of Zanskar, claims to be eighty-one. It is he who saw the yeti, or *tedmo*, as it is called here. Too old now to toil in the fields, he works at home, engraving mantras on stone slabs. The engraved stones are known as *mani* stones and are set at the entrance to a village, where they form sacred walls announcing the Buddha's *chörtens*.

Fragile enclave in time and space, Zanskar is permeated in its day-to-day life by the Tibetan religion. The ancient kingdom of Zanskar was dependent upon Ladakh and Tibet; since 1842 it has belonged to the Muslim Indian state of Jammu and Kashmir. Between May and November a dirt road connects its ancient capital, Padum, with the centre of local government, the Islamic town of Kargil (a two-day journey from Padum by lorry). While their borders are slowly being eaten away by the expansionist aims of the Kashmiris, who are the dominant force in commerce and administration throughout the state, the people of Zanskar cling to their Tibetan language and to the system of values which has enabled them to survive in their high, wild valleys since the seventh century.

They can still be reached only on foot, at the price of an eight- to ten-day climb over the high passes. That is unless one shoots down the frozen river in January – seventy-odd miles down a canyon from which one would never escape alive if there were a sudden thaw.

Tomtches and his six sons are afraid of nothing. Traditionally, the eldest son marries, becomes head of the family and inherits the lands and the house. A novice at seven, the second son is destined to be a monk; the rest remain at home with the eldest. They share everything, even the one wife. This custom of polyandry, which prevents the parcelling out of precious arable land by limiting the number of births, is honoured throughout the Himalayan region; but it no longer survives where technological development has introduced other life-styles and new sources of income.

Thus, Tomtches's second son, Sonam Phuntsok, aged thirty-one, is not a monk, but a soldier in the Ladakhi regiment based in Leh. Norges, Tzering Lobsang (twenty-four) and Tentzing Namtak (twenty-one) add spice to their lives through numerous conquests rather than sharing the common marriage bed. And it was out of personal choice that Tzewang Norbu, the youngest, entered the monastery of Karsha.

Once married, the eldest son, Garshung, left to bring up his three children in a neighbouring house – a further departure from tradition. Tomtches and his wife Norbu Iche have stayed on with their younger sons instead of moving to a smaller house as Memele and great-grandmother Abele ('grandmother') Sonam Pele have done.

Despite their advanced age, these two are still active. Last autumn Memele hewed the shaft of a hoe with a hatchet; at the beginning of June, as soon as the last ice has melted, Tomtches and Norges will attach it to two yaks and work the barley field with it.

The younger children go up to the high pastures with the yaks and the *dzos*, a cross between the cow and the yak. These animals constitute the family riches. They provide everything: milk, yoghurt, cheese, butter and dung, and, finally, meat and leather. On the roof and walls of the mountain huts, cheeses and cakes of dung dry side by side in preparation for the winter, while the store room fills with huge pats of strong-smelling butter wrapped in yak skin.

On occasion, some of these good Buddhists will even turn to a bit of hunting. Since they are not allowed to take life themselves, killing a goat or a sheep requires that they wait patiently until a helpful Muslim passes by.... But how to resist an encounter with an ibex, or one of its cousins, the bharal or the urial? The marmot and the fox are easier to track; the snow leopard and especially the wolf, the *chankou*, are very secretive and greatly feared. The numerous traps – deep, cone-shaped pits ringed with a low wall – in the vicinity of villages and mountain pastures attest the presence of the latter.

In the plain, Iche and her daughter-in-law grow a few onions, cabbages and, particularly, peas, a rare delicacy to be savoured one by one. There are just these few vegetables in Zanskar, and no fruit at all. Two young girls watch over the irrigation. Each village has a system of grass-grown channels which carry water from the mountain streams to the fields. As much fodder as possible is harvested in order to feed the yaks, *dzos*, goats and sheep through the winter.

In September the services of the entire family are requisitioned. Norges gives up his romantic excursions, Norbu quits the monastery, Sonam obtains leave of absence, and they all go off to the fields with a sickle in their hands.

The women harvest the barley on their knees, ear by ear if necessary. Once the crop has dried, Tomtches and his sons drive a stake into the ground. Round this stake the animals turn, tirelessly trampling the ears of barley to the rhythm of a high-pitched chant; for, as they throw the grain up in the air, the workers pipe a shrill and monotonous tune. One peasant sings behind his yaks, another whistles to call the wind, and so between them they perform a musical duet which fills the terraced fields at the end of September.

It will be Abele's job to mount guard on the flat roof of the house and to scare the birds away from the barley that has been spread out to dry there. Iche and the women will roast some of it and take the rest to the water mill. But they won't neglect to set aside a generous portion for making *chang*. *Chang*, or barley beer, is simply the product of barleycorn left to ferment in water. The women mash it until it reaches that slightly viscous consistency which gives the ice-cold liquid its aroma and just the right degree of potency to liven up the evenings. It requires two or three degrees, no more: the altitude accentuates the effects of the alcohol. When the harvest is a particularly good one, Tomtches and his sons become home distillers and produce a hearty brew called *arak*. This is the prelude to really good drinking times to come! For the harsher the living conditions, the more lively the festivities.... Zanskar is the country of *joie de vivre*. As long as the stocks of *chang* last, occasions for merry-making follow one upon another throughout the winter.

Tomtches's house in Pishu is always full of visitors: relations, neighbours and friends from other villages. These sedentary peasants are restless. They may not often venture far from home – Kargil is 'Muslim country' and Kashmir a foreign land – but they come and go within their valleys. If a wooden post is needed for the house, Norges and Tomtches will think nothing of going three days on foot to fetch one, across the impressive bridge of ropes and creepers suspended over the seething river, and up steep paths sometimes no broader than a foot's width. They will stop off at a friend's house on the way, and be welcomed there as warmly as visitors are in their own home.

The guest is ritually offered, first, sweet tea, of which he will accept only one cup, since sugar is a precious commodity; then salty buttered tea, the famous sour drink of the Himalayas, a source of warmth, salt and fat indispensable to survival. If it is a mealtime, *tsampa* is dipped in the tea; *tsampa*, a paste of roasted barley, is also useful for wiping one's bowl clean before putting it away in the folds of one's *goncha*. *Tsampa* cakes are also eaten, and *tsampa* soup; while on especially propitious days, there is *mok-mok*, *tsampa* 'ravioli', stuffed with meat or cabbage.

Then there is more barley, this time in the form of *chang*, which flows liberally, though in measured quantities: Iche pours little at a time, but keeps on pouring. In the evening, the little wooden, china or silver bowls are never empty as long as the conversation lasts. The weather-beaten faces, deeply etched and lined, light up and soften. The people of Zanskar are always smiling; they are a profoundly gentle people.

In winter, when the snow-shrouded valleys are deathly still and silent, the whole family lives in a single room, surrounded by the stables, at the heart of the house. The smoke is scarcely able to escape through the tiny aperture left for the purpose; they believe that it also helps to keep them warm. During more than six months of the year, eighteen hours a day are spent hibernating in this way, often in a temperature only just above freezing, while outside it may be as low as −30°C (−22°F). Tomtches and his family only let the animals out at the end of the morning, when the sun has had a chance to warm the air. They clean out the stables, go and break the ice and fetch some water. Around midday, the neighbours get together and sit against a wall in the sun to have a chat while their children play. Then everyone returns to huddle once more around the fire.

This is the time when the evil spirits are abroad. No one ventures outside, or even opens the door, after nightfall in case one of the spirits has assumed the appearance of a relative or neighbour. In Zanskar ancient beliefs still hold sway, inspiring the tales and legends told round the fire at night.

Then silence descends. This is the moment for reflection. Grandfather's chanting of the sacred mantra *Om mani padme hum* can be heard in counterpoint to the crackling of the fire. The *chang* is brought out, then the *arak*. Laughter and songs start up again until, all fairly tipsy, the family lie down where they are to sleep, on the beaten earth, sandwiched between mats and blankets.

To combat the boredom of such a long winter, Norges and various other young men go off on expeditions together. They climb the ridges in search of dead tree stumps, which they root up and bring home to hang as trophies round the edges of the flat roofs. With wood in such cruelly short supply, these stumps are symbols of prosperity, preserved all the more proudly for their rarity. The peasants plant willows with their children in mind: to serve as beams in the houses that their offspring will build in twenty years' time. . . . Though its slopes may be covered in edelweiss and blue poppies, the whole of Zanskar boasts only a handful of thickets and six old trees. One of them, held to be sacred, towers over the monastery of Phuctal, the spiritual apogee of the ancient kingdom.

Fifty or sixty monks live there. Their cells cling to the sheer rock face and form a cluster of white cubes beneath the sacred grotto where a holy man lived in about the seventh century. As in all Zanskar's monasteries, there are two types of monk, one religious, the other secular. The former study and meditate, conduct the services and, under the direction of the Tibetan Grand Master sent by the Dalai Lama, analyse in depth the Buddhist texts. The other monks are there only by reason of being younger sons, rather than by vocation. They work in the fields, maintain the buildings or engage in trading.

The richest monastery in Zanskar, Karsha, has large areas of land, numerous herds of animals and a well-stocked shop at its disposal. Buddhists are practical people, well aware of practical necessities. The tithe system may have disappeared, but the monks do not live cut off from the rest of the world; they go back to their families for the harvest and return in the autumn, well supplied with provisions for the winter.

It is in the monasteries that the entire population gathers for the most important festival of the year, *Gostor*. At this occasion, religious services and lamaistic dances, with elaborate masks and costumes, alternate with traditional dances of an entirely profane character. Engagements are celebrated and the new couples dance before the crowd to the sound of drums and oboes. While the New Year festival is a local village affair, *Gostor* is *the* social event of the year: distant family members are reunited, news is swapped and romances are started. It is there too that business deals are transacted. The peasants from the upper valleys arrive laden with butter from their high mountain pastures and organize caravans to take their produce down the frozen river and sell it in Leh. Letters and messages are exchanged and then relayed by the travellers from house to house, since the Indian postal service does not extend to the villages but stops at the chief town, Padum.

Although the capital of Zanskar, Padum is, in reality, scarcely even a little country town. Besides its thousand inhabitants, it has an administrative officer, a sad young Indian doctor obliged to spend his three post-study years there, four soldiers equipped with one walkie-talkie, a few shops – and Zanskar's one and only television set.

This is the end of the road which, one day, will extend to the villages, thereby affecting the way of life of the entire population. Meanwhile, in Zanskar the industrial revolution means the little cast-iron oven which makes the kitchen less smoky; the spirit stove which saves on wood; the storm lantern, and, of course, the battery: life is transformed by the existence of pocket torches and radios.... Later there will be electricity. Padum and Karsha already have a diesel-run generator which lights up the bare bulbs in the kitchens until nine or ten at night – without a switch: people go to sleep when the official in charge decides to stop the motor.

So few things have changed. One that has is schooling. The Indian administration is starting up classes and Tomtches's children will learn Urdu and a little English. Some of the boys are studying in Leh and in Srinagar. The outside world is getting nearer. Two monks have left the monastery at Phuctal, in order to join the army: sign of the times! Four or five families in Padum are calling their house a 'hotel' and taking in tourists.

Zanskar is gradually opening up. Through the medium of television and contact with foreigners, it is discovering a world which is in many respects incomprehensible but which it nevertheless accepts – without being overly envious of it. The trekkers' sophisticated equipment is regarded with more admiration than longing; and if the women and children beg, they are asking only for sweets, soap or pencils. Not for money – not yet.

But the country is changing in profound ways. There is no rightful successor to the throne now that the two old kings are dead; no one to assume the role of guarantor of the social and moral order. And so the last words of the king of Padum to Olivier Föllmi are coming true: 'Don't be sad. In Zanskar we have always followed the teachings of Buddha. Those teachings are based on the transience of all things. It's part of the natural order that Zanskar should change.'

Jacques Poget

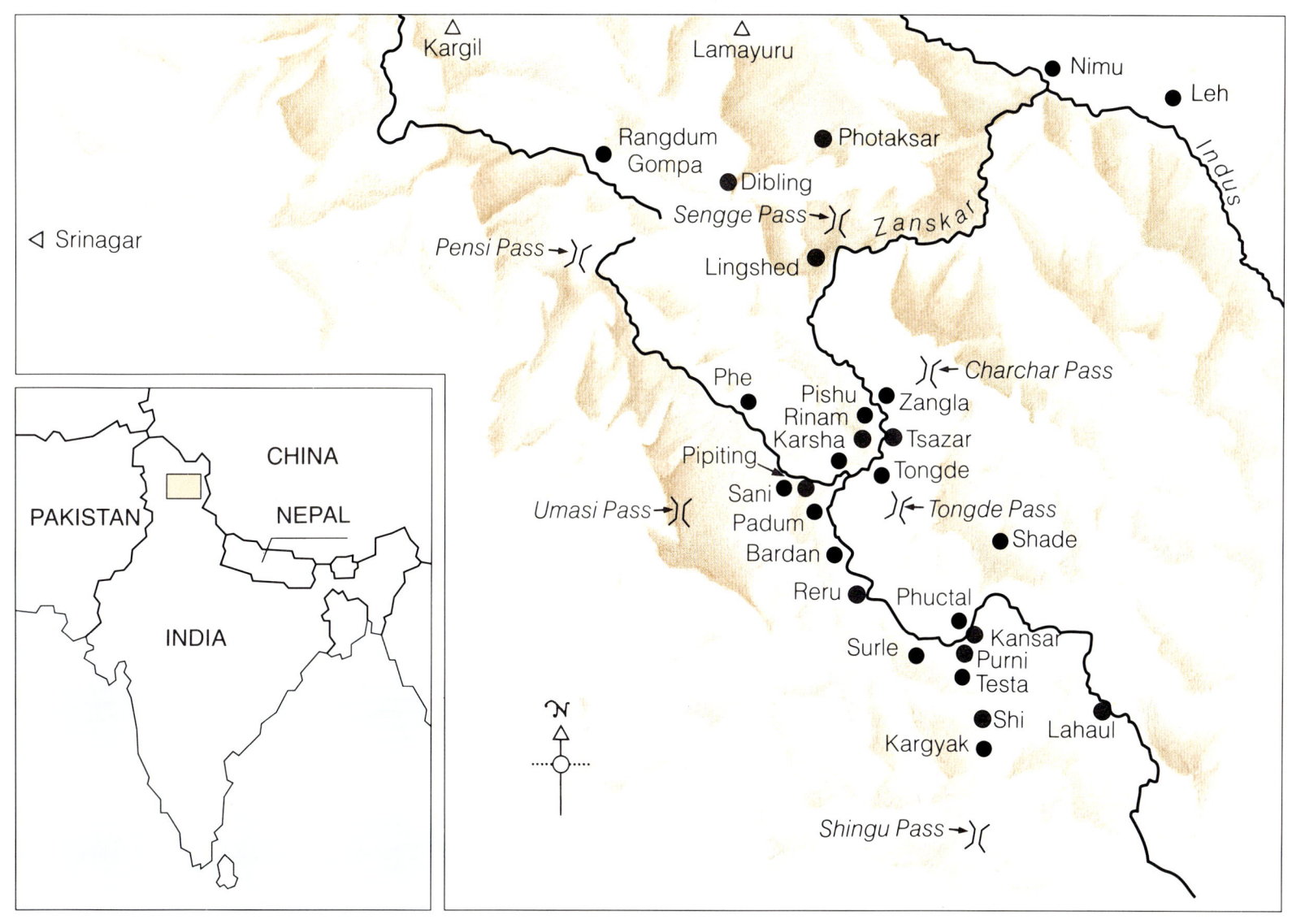

For Dolma, for the laughter and tears we shared,
Daskit, for your goat torn to pieces by the wolves,
Tundup, for your lesson about the stars in Tantak cave,
Yangkit, for having woven me the woollen cloak,
Meme Geshe, the old master who hovers daily over the monastery,
Nawang, for all the rivers we crossed,
Kusang, for your strength-giving soup,
Memele, for having chased away the yeti,
Tashi, for your chanting in the firelight,
Pedma, for the calmness of your gaze,
Phuntsok, for the god that resides in your goat,
Tzering, for our gallop to the village,
Toyot, for your shining eyes over the chang bowl,
Tashi Namgyel Gyalpo, content to die and continue his journey,
Lamo, for the snare set to trap the evil spirits,
Lobsang, my companion through life for a while,
Palden, for your offerings to the god of travellers when last I left,
Dorje, for our dance at the monastery,
Stenzing, for our moments of silence,
        . . . for the beauty of your smiles, Djulle'Dju!

Olivier

7

8

Zanskar's paths are blocked by ice eight months of the year, and precipices, torrential streams and storms over the passes make them particularly hazardous. Each year the caravans lose a number of animals, and sometimes men too. In the winter, snow leopards roam near the villages and slink into the cattle sheds. One summer morning, Daskit's goat disappeared from the Tahang fields. His father was worried and went out to bring in the rest of the herd. But he found his twelve goats torn to pieces by the wolves. His horse was also badly wounded in the hindquarters and had to be brought back to the stable and fed with hay. Lobsang owned half the animal (the hind part), his brother-in-law the other half (the head and forequarters); but since the hindquarters were at present immobilizing the whole horse, Lobsang was obliged to feed both halves at his own expense.

10

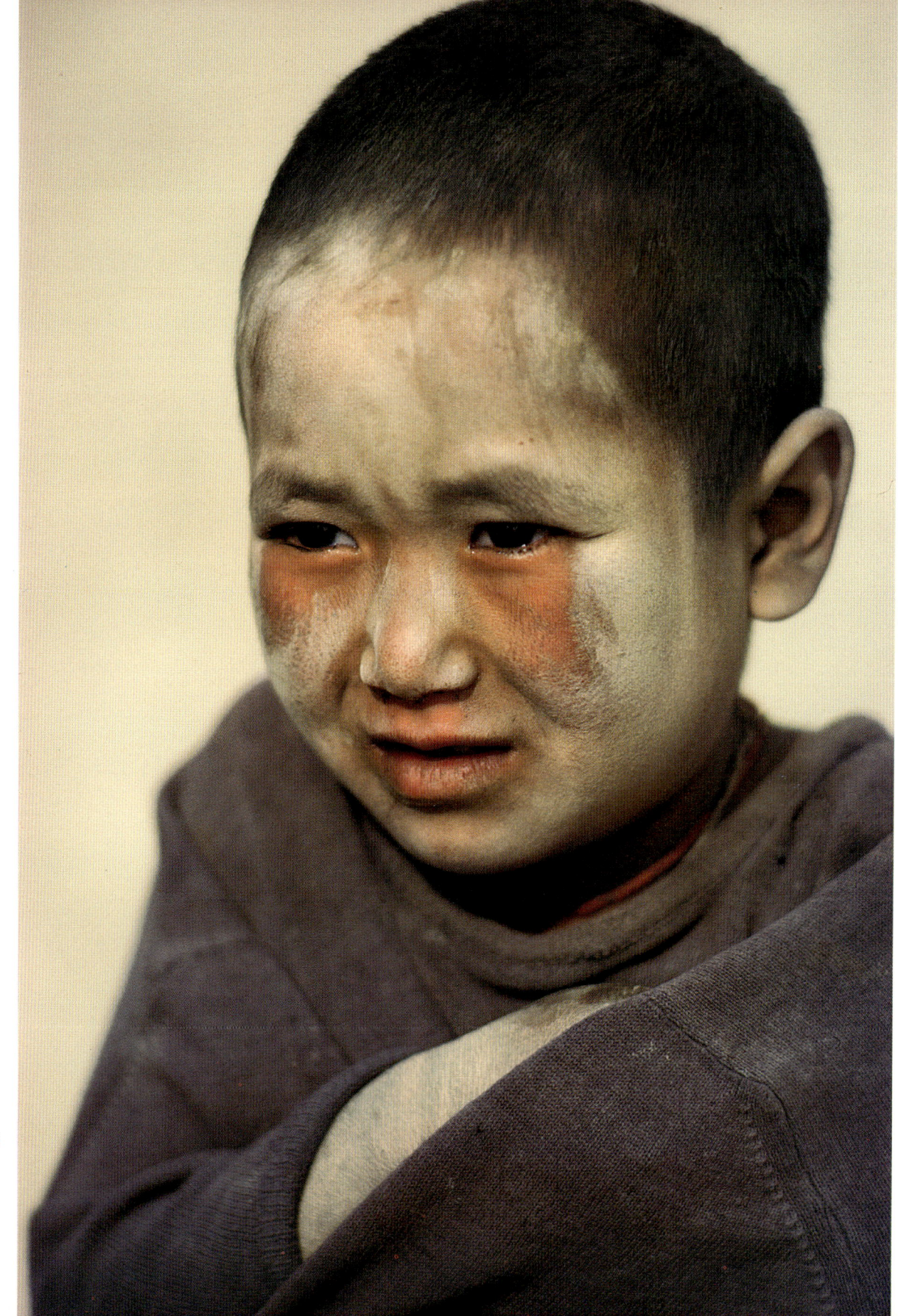

In Zanskar people always call each other 'big brother' or 'little sister'; they have no surnames. A spiritual grand master chooses the children's first name. One day, Nawang Phuntsok went to meet the Dalai Lama and bring back a name for his son, a journey of eighteen days on foot. On his return to the village, he wished to celebrate the granting of such a lucky name. The villagers decided to kill a goat and make mok-moks. But being Buddhists, none of them could actually kill the animal. Phuntsok, four of his neighbours and I went down to the path which caravans sometimes take, in the hope of meeting a Muslim trader who could kill our goat for us. We drank chang and waited in the shade of a chörten, but five hours went by without our seeing a soul. In the end, Phuntsok deduced from this that his goat was sacred and that it wasn't meant to die. We went back up to the village, feeling full of respect for the animal, and that evening we fed it cabbage mok-moks, which it ate with us in the kitchen. Since then the goat has been treated with reverence and regarded as the protector of Stensing Löfen, Nawang Phuntsok's son.

19

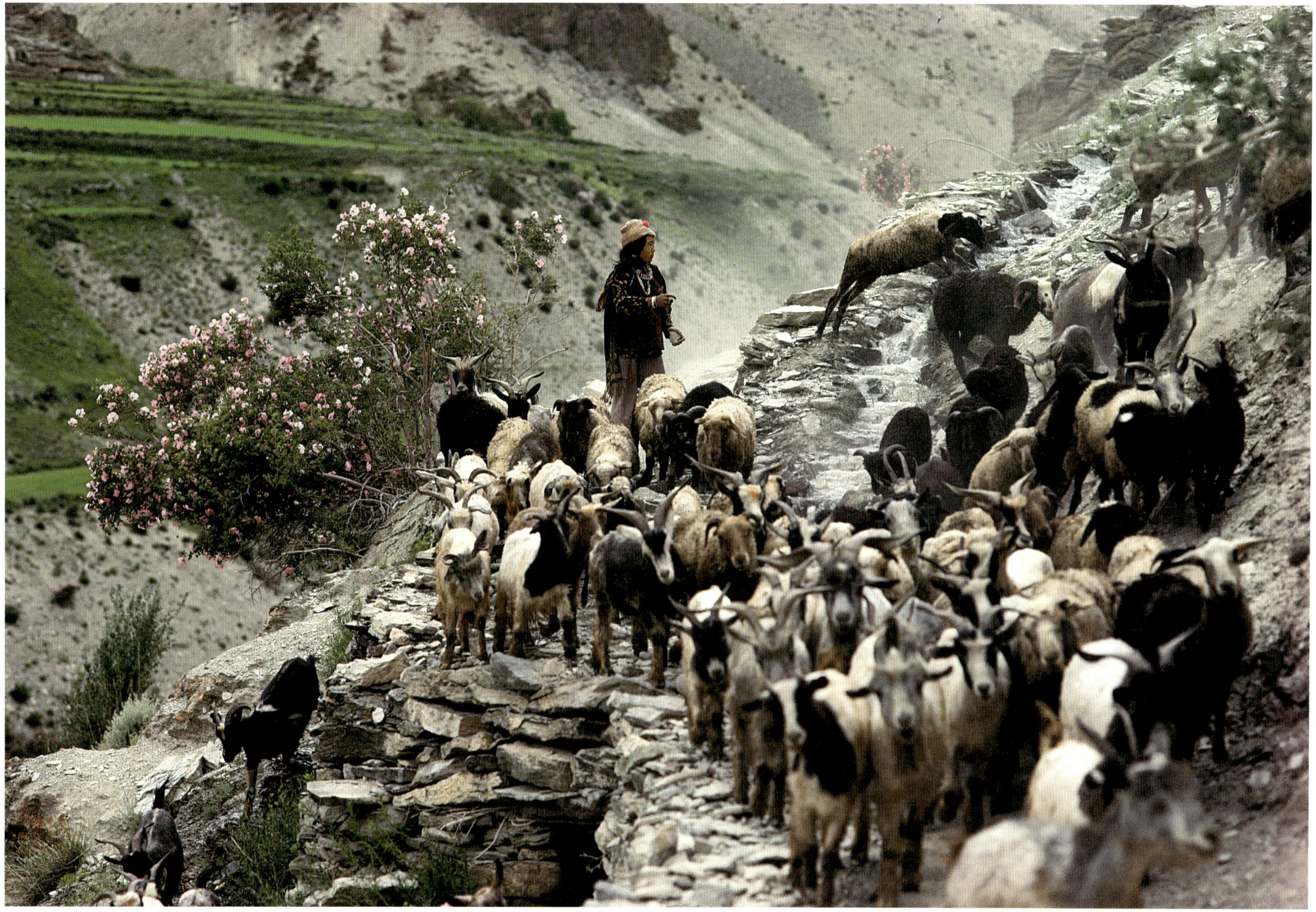

20

21

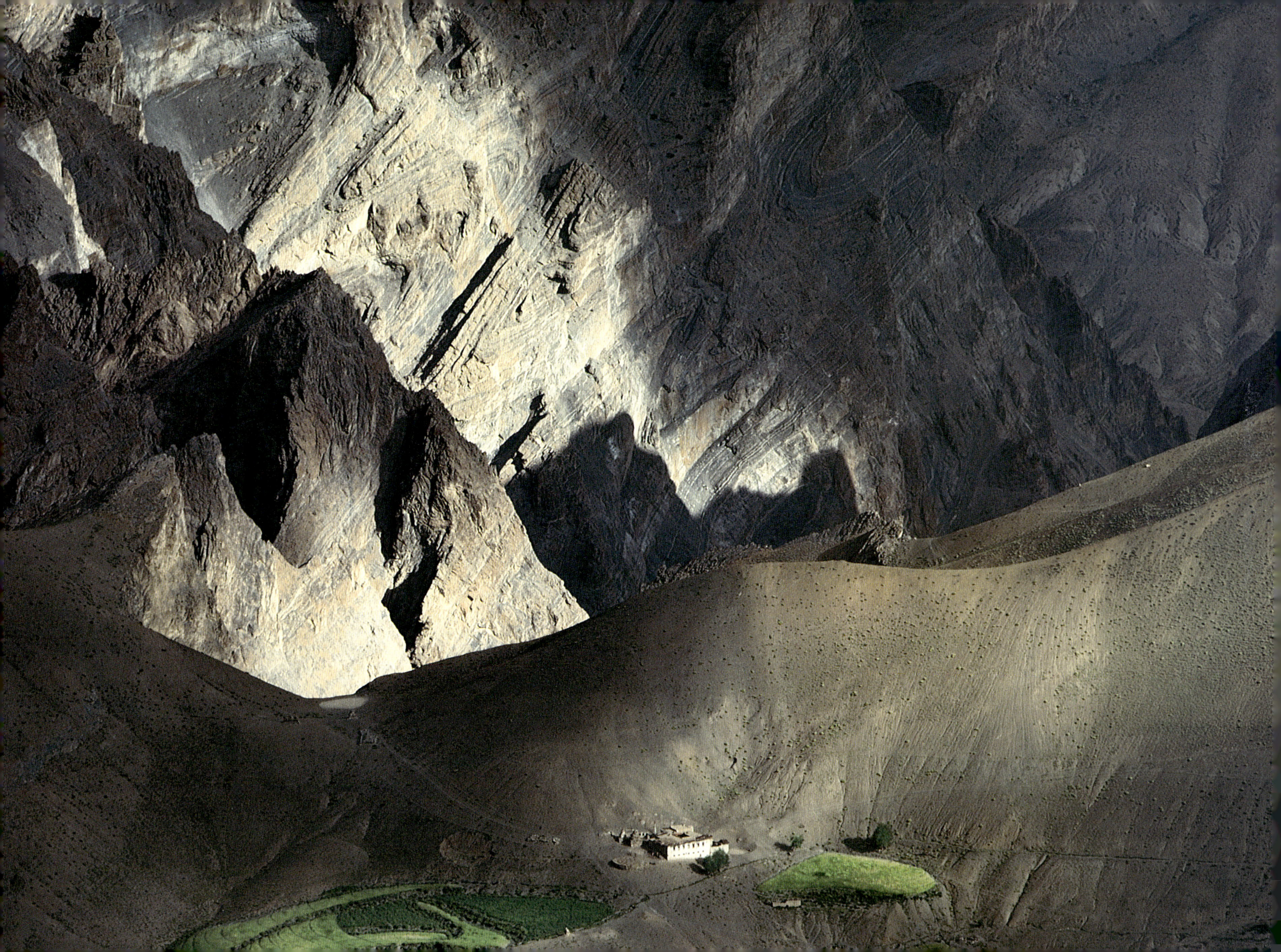

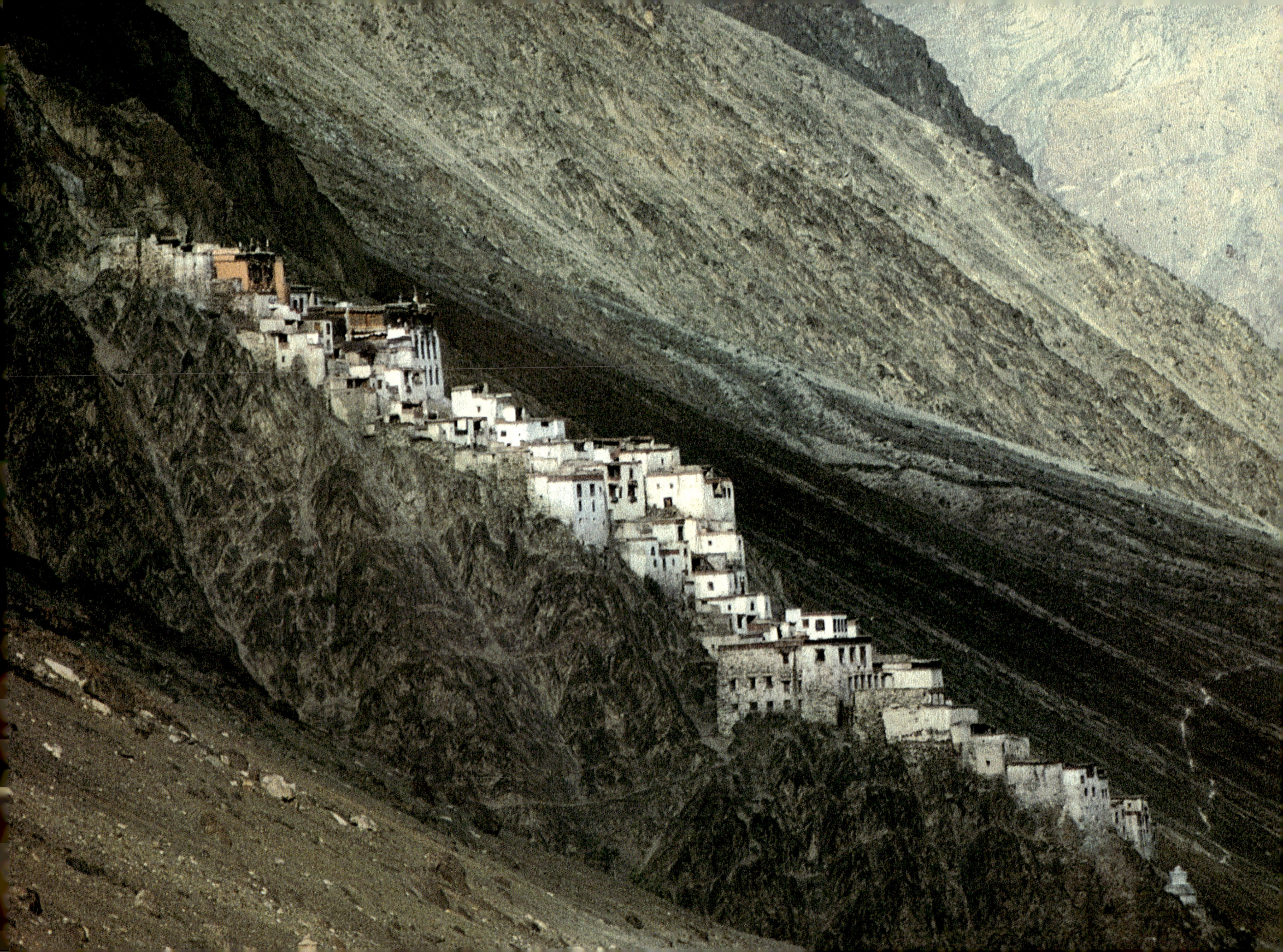

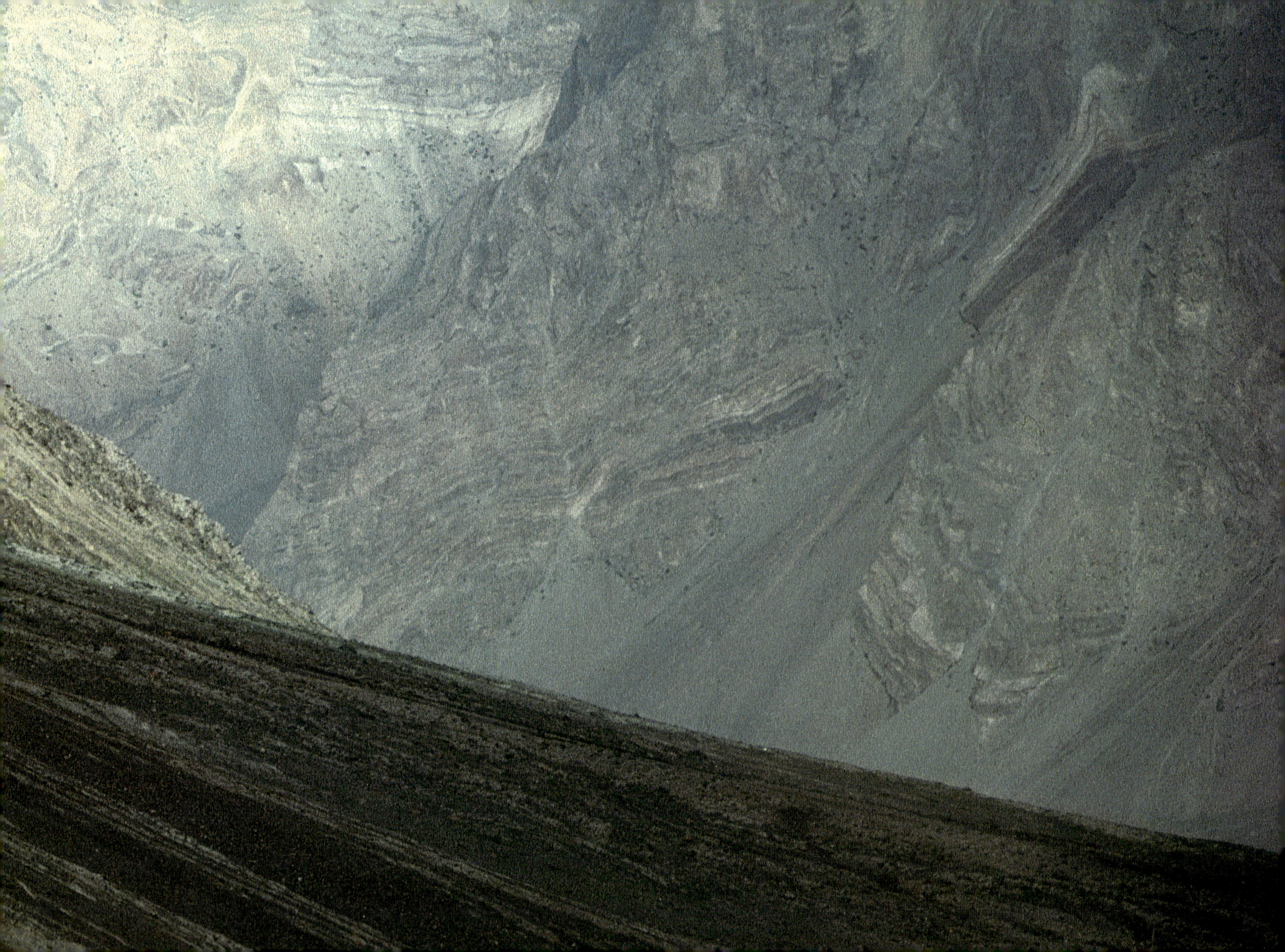

24

25

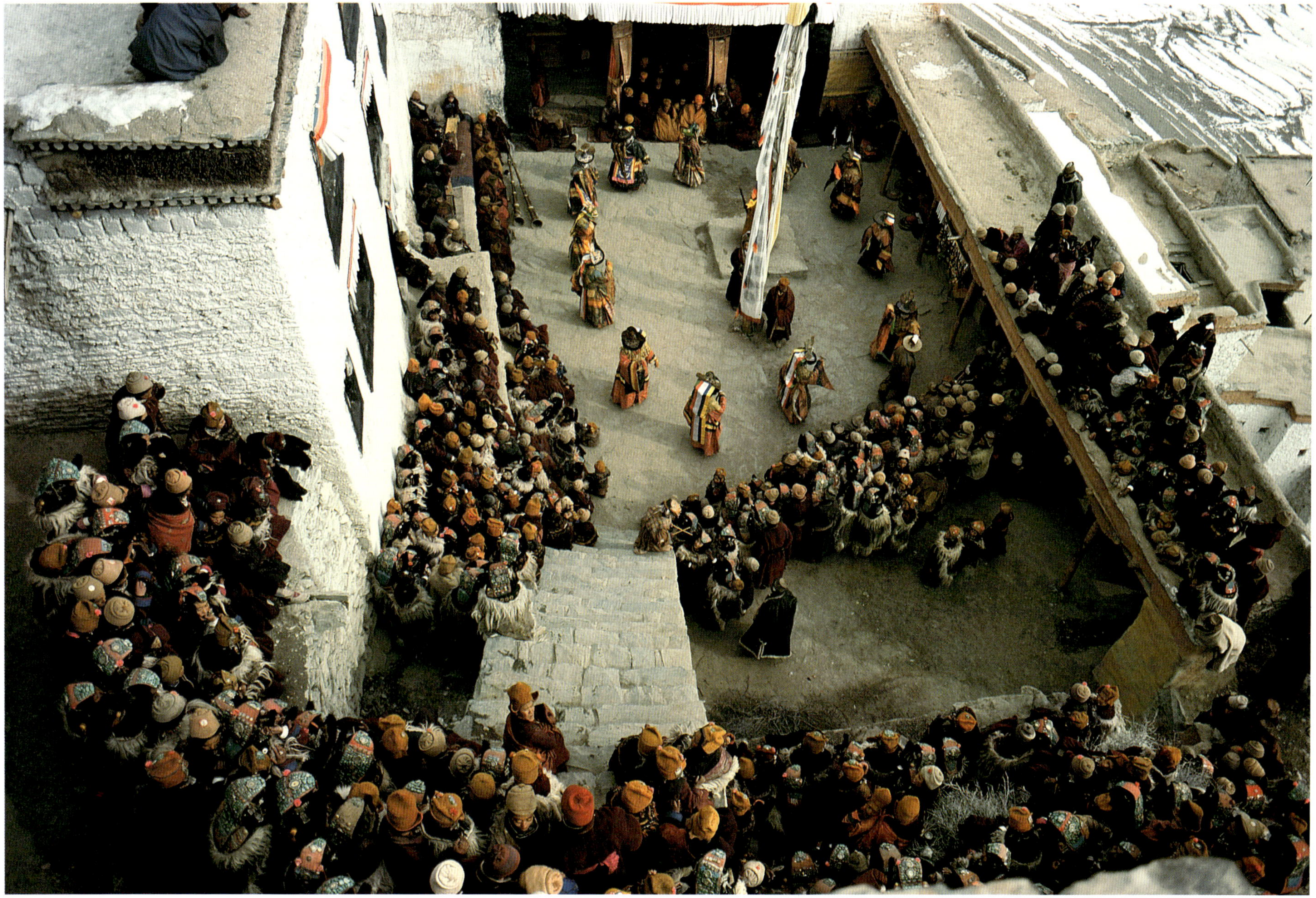

28

29

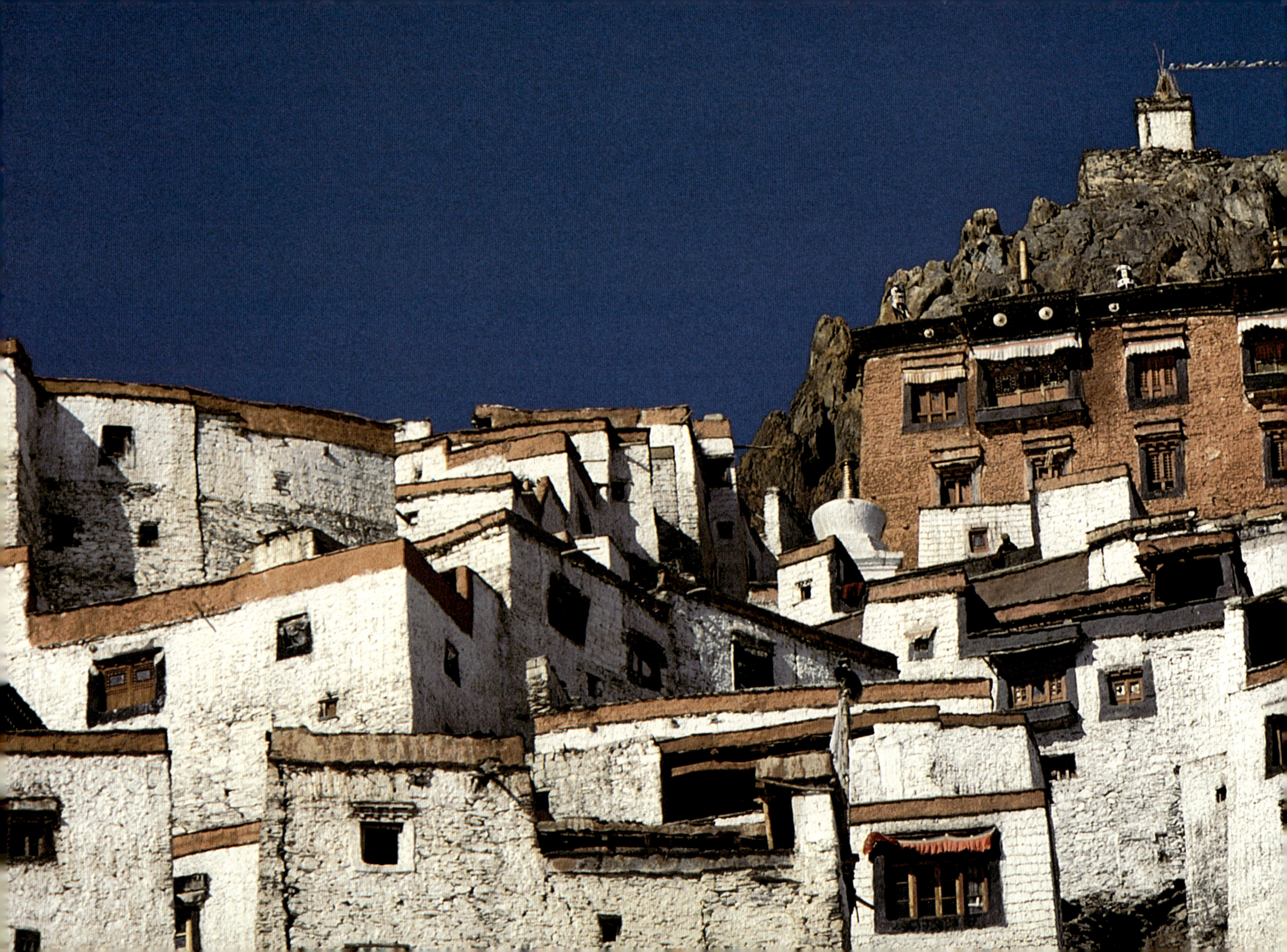

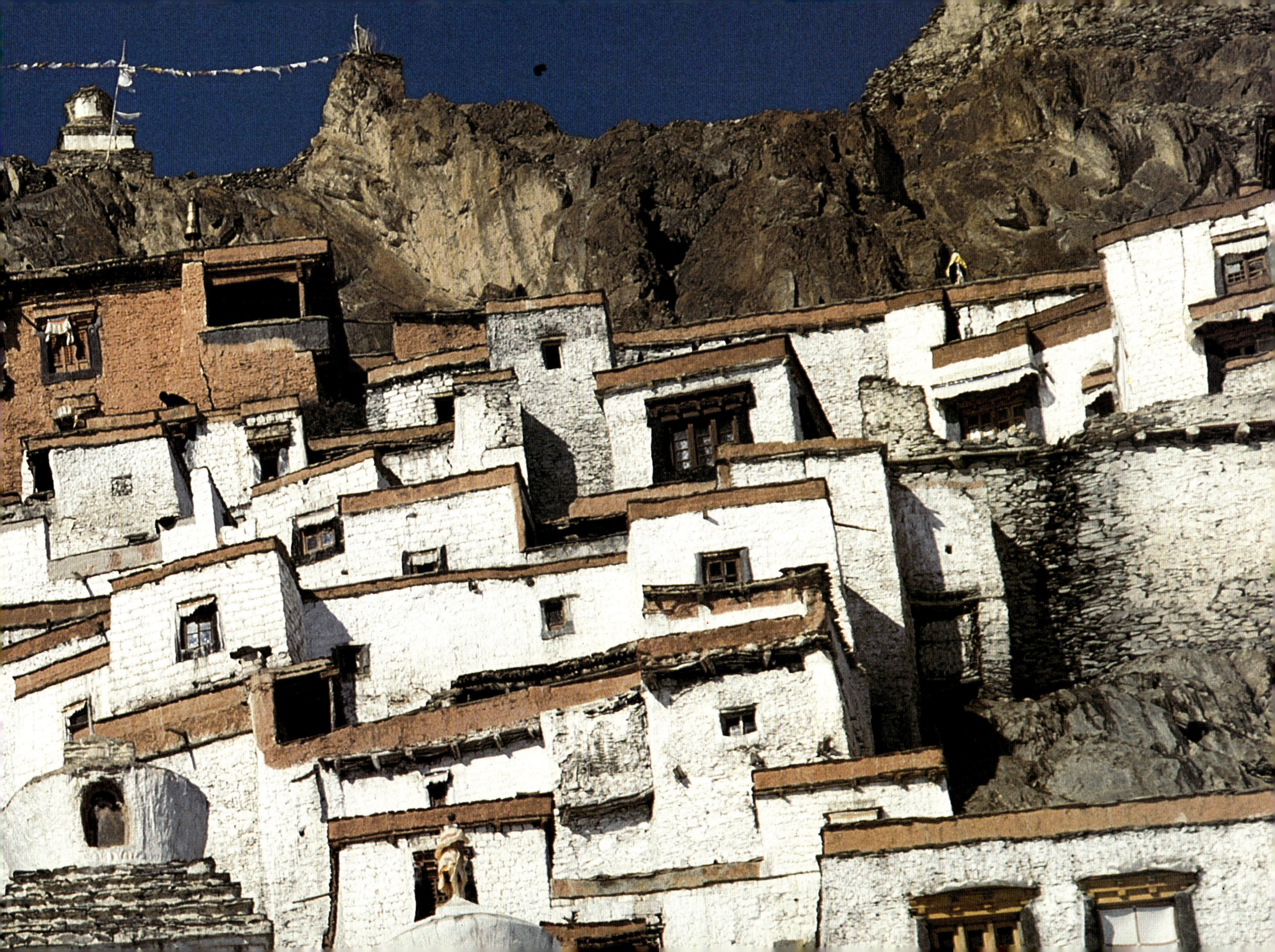

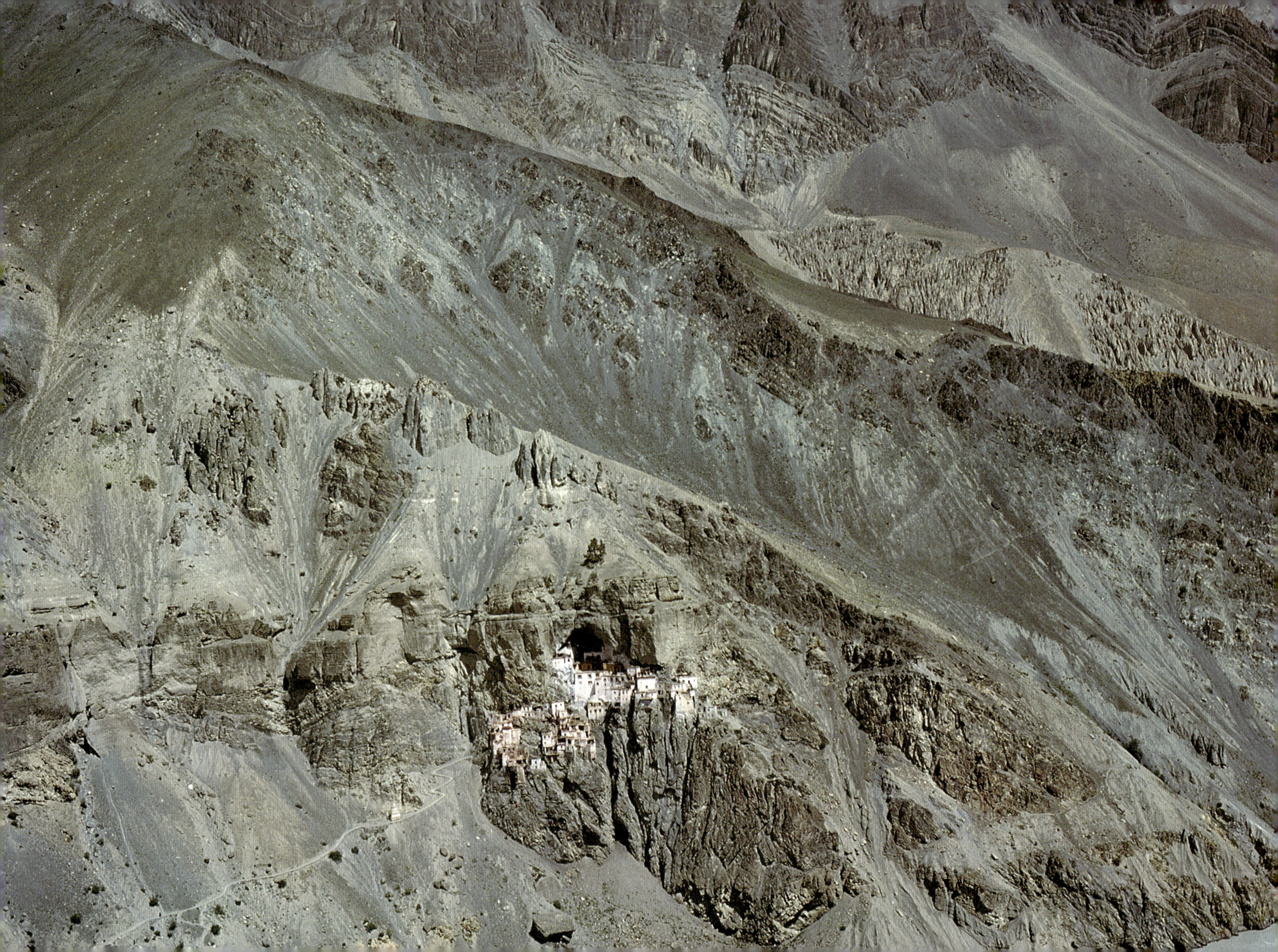

The third bend in the river is the territory of the monk who flies. His monastery is perched high up on the rock wall and the approaches are littered with droppings white as lime. Each morning he flies to the lake, the mirror of the gods. The Phuctal monks place offerings of barley-flour pellets at the foot of his retreat, and the caravan on its way to Yarshun pitches camp beneath the wall in order to benefit through the night from the auspicious influence of this holy place. This is, it seems, the reincarnation in the form of an eagle of an old hermit who used to meditate in Tantak cave. He sometimes comes and hovers over the monastery and, with his wings, greets the monks praying on the terrace. He is known as Meme Geshe, 'Venerable Old Master'.

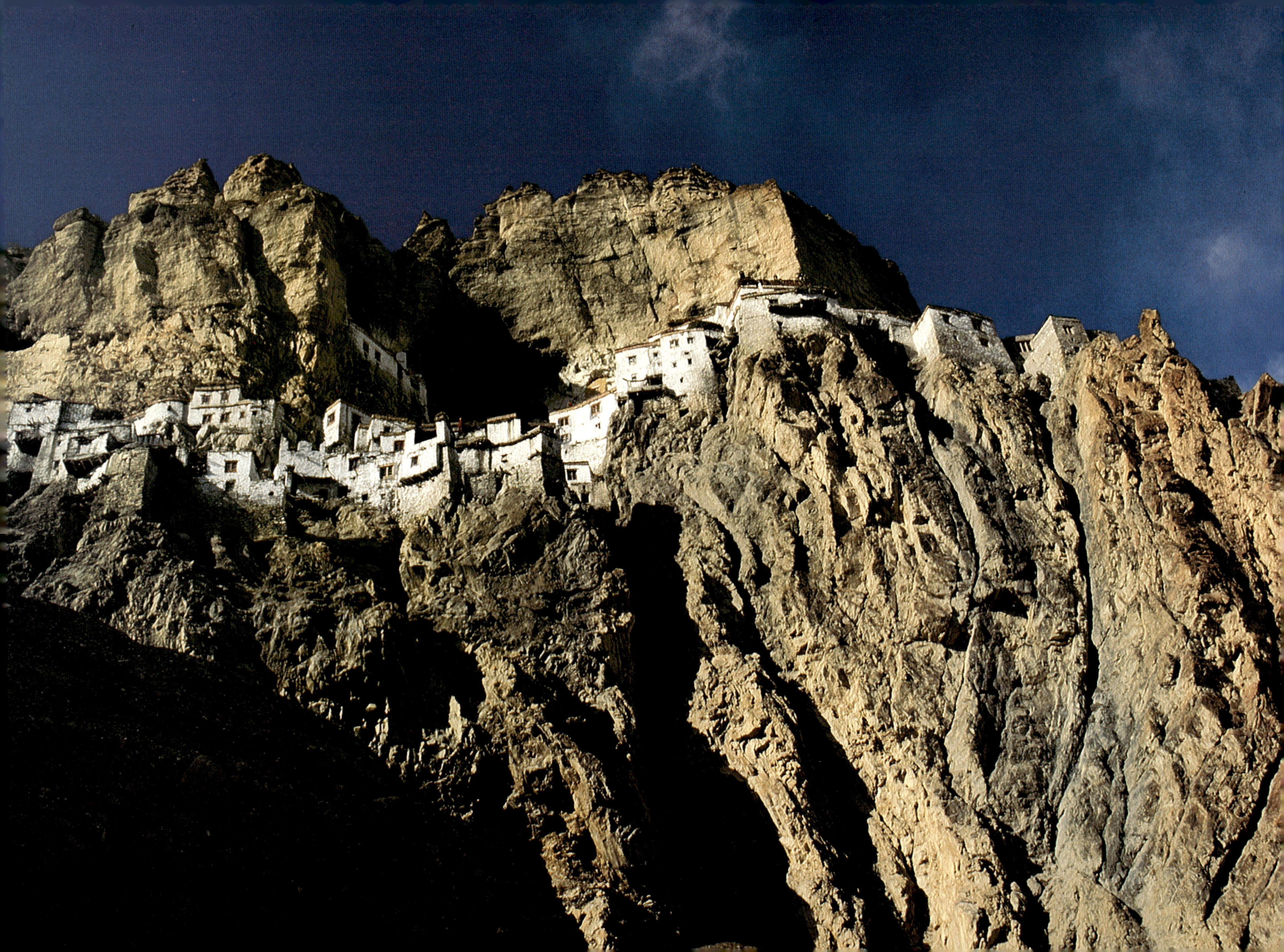

33

34

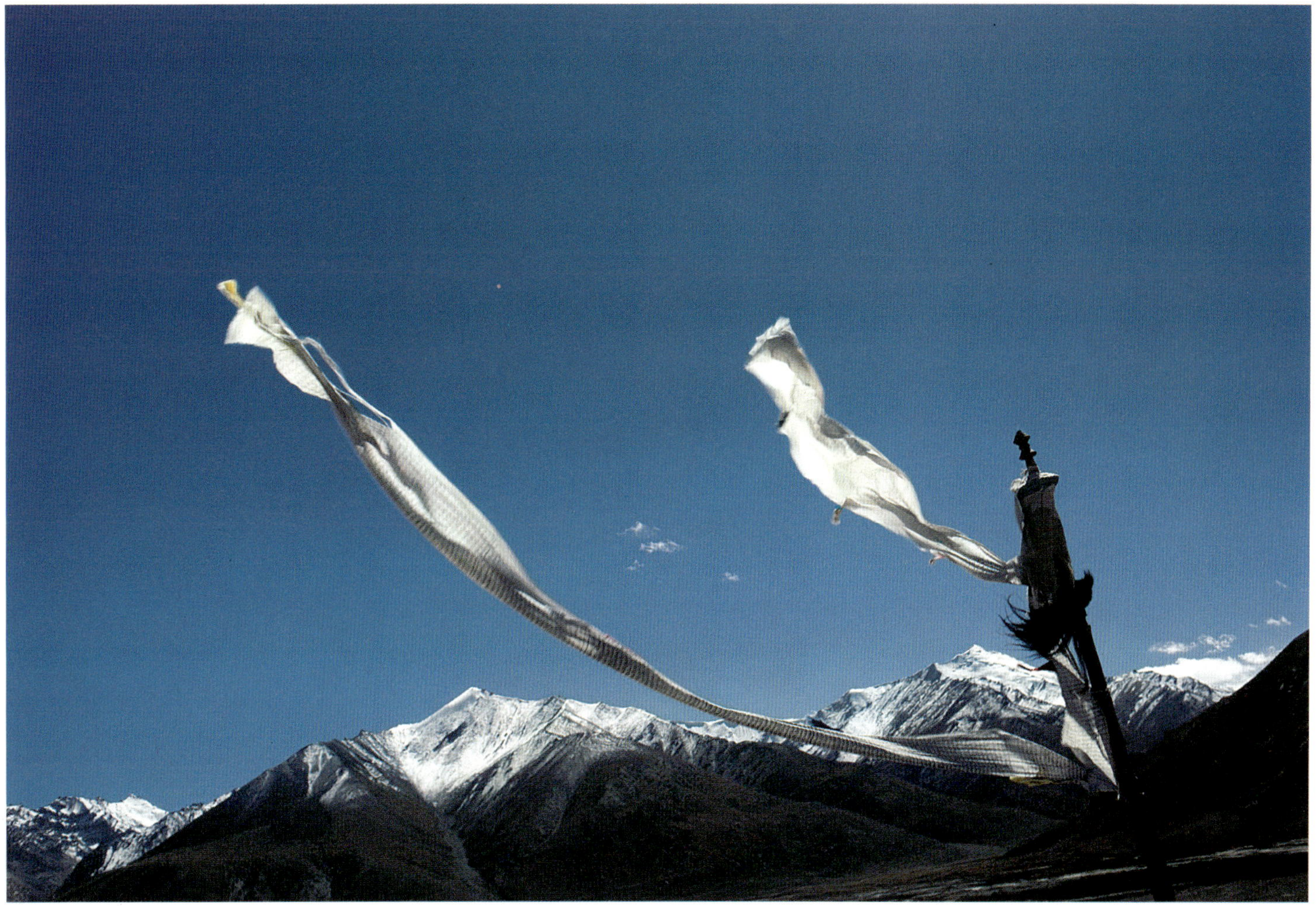

35

36

37

8

39

40

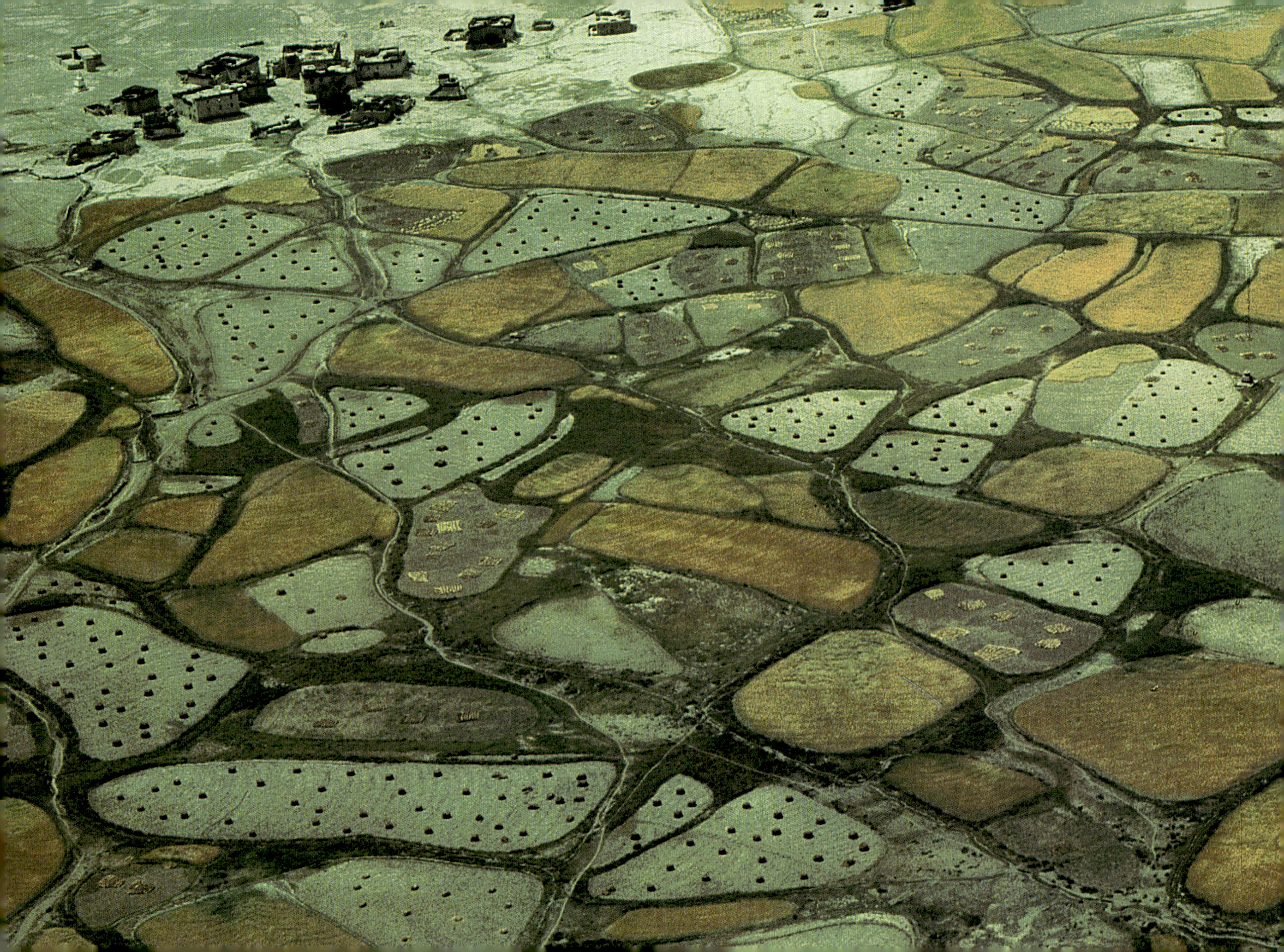

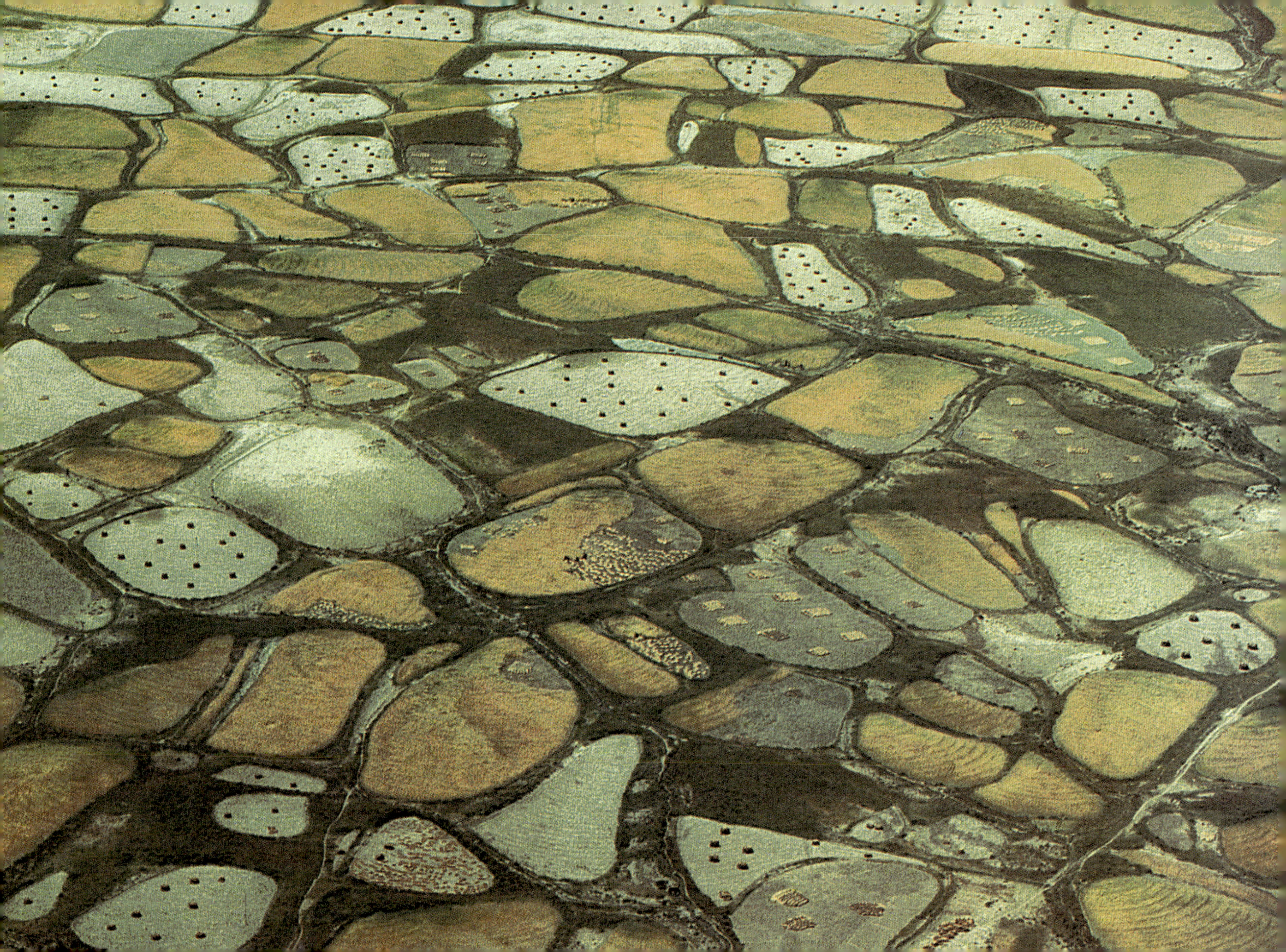

42

43

The Zanskari name for the yeti is tedmo. In Pishu the children frequently ask grandfather Memele to tell the story of how, at eighty-one, he saw the yeti in the village one day during the harvest. The tedmo is about three feet tall and walks like a man. It is harmless when going downhill because its long hair covers its eyes. Going uphill, on the other hand, when it pushes the strands of hair back off its face, it is dangerous.

Memele was praying in front of the house in the sun. The tedmo came up and was about to break down the stable door, but Memele brandished his stick at it and chased it off as far as the river. Since then, Memele has prayed at the entrance to his stable.

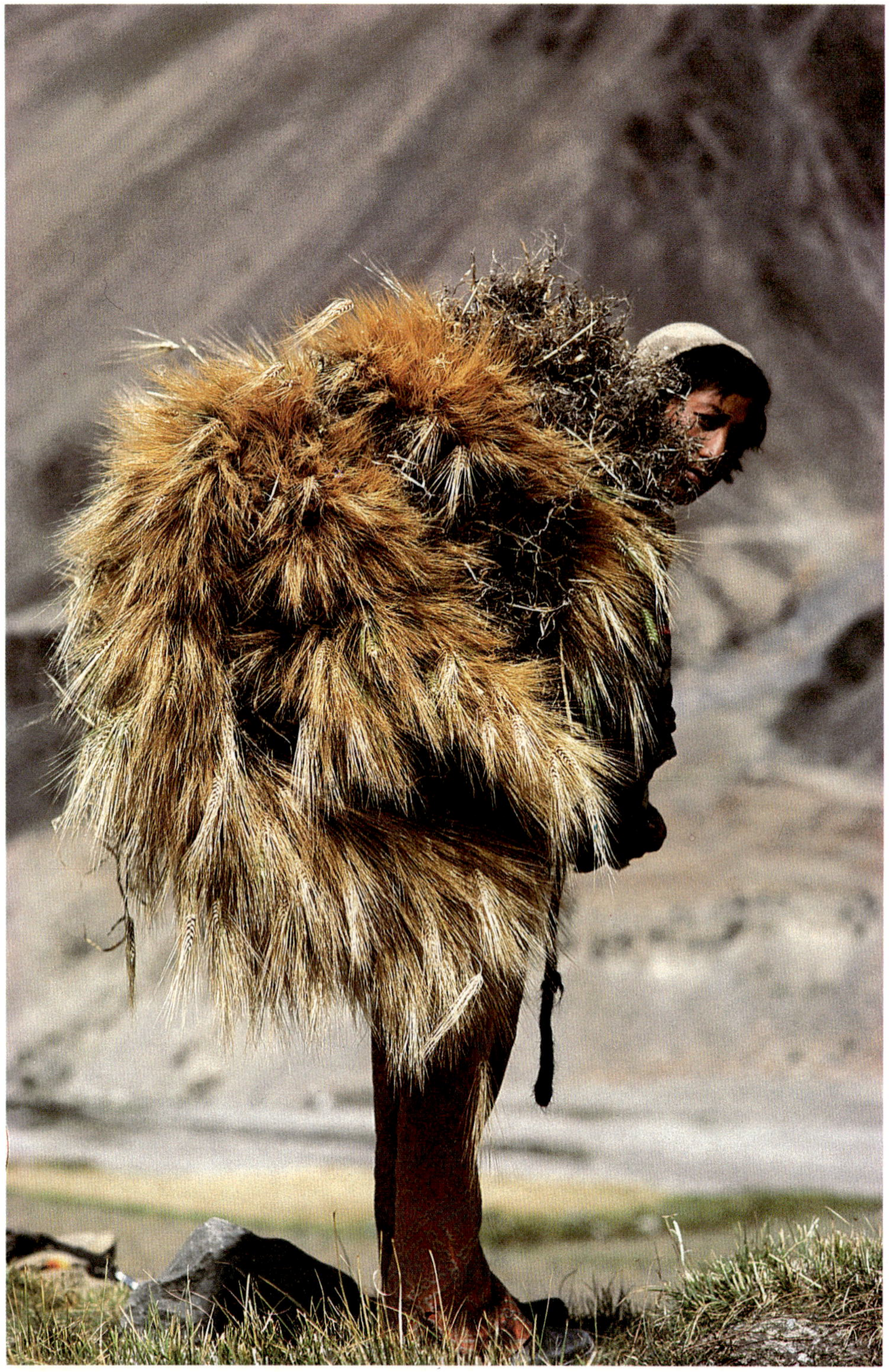

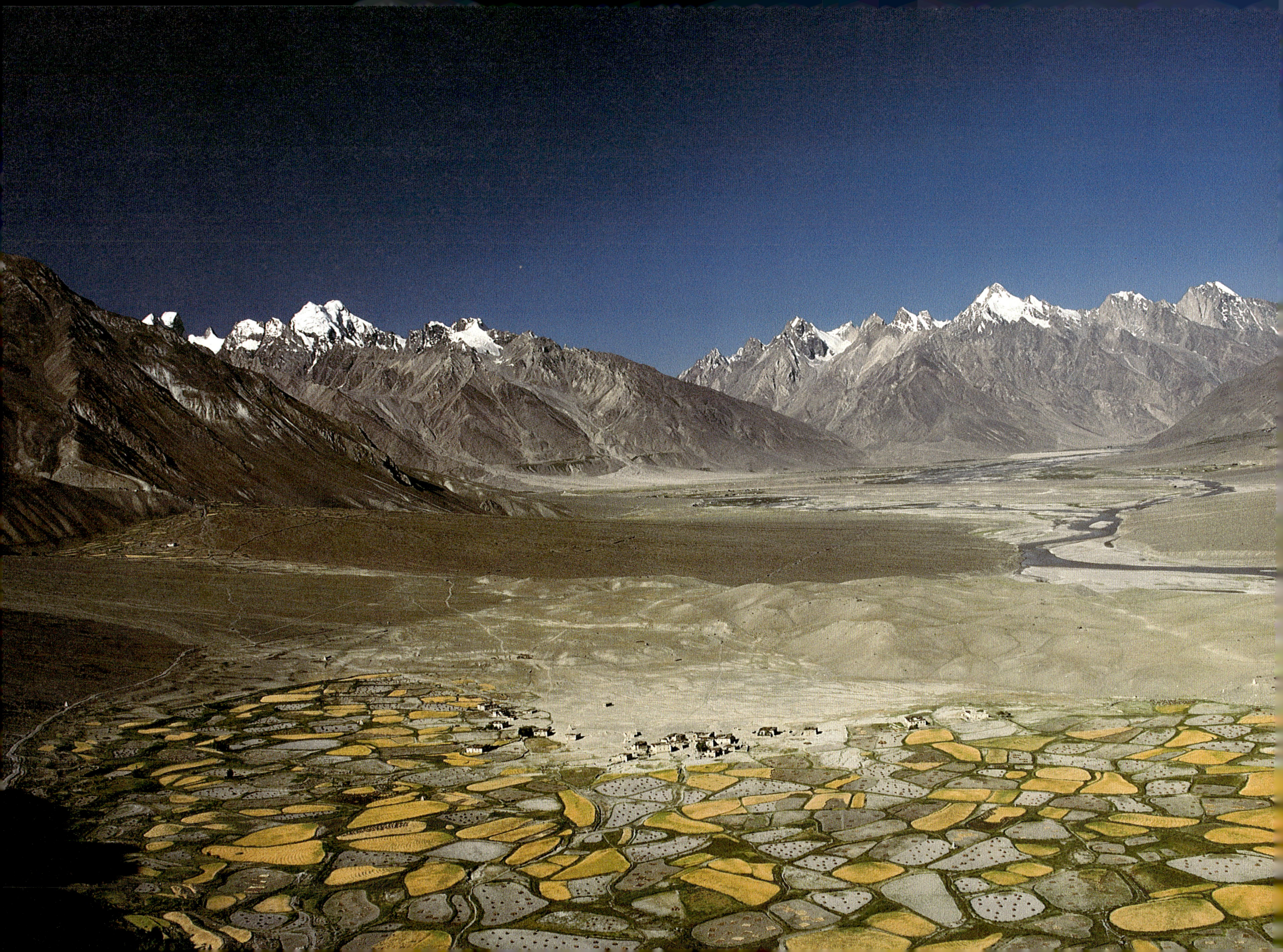

48

49

50

51

52

53

54

55 56

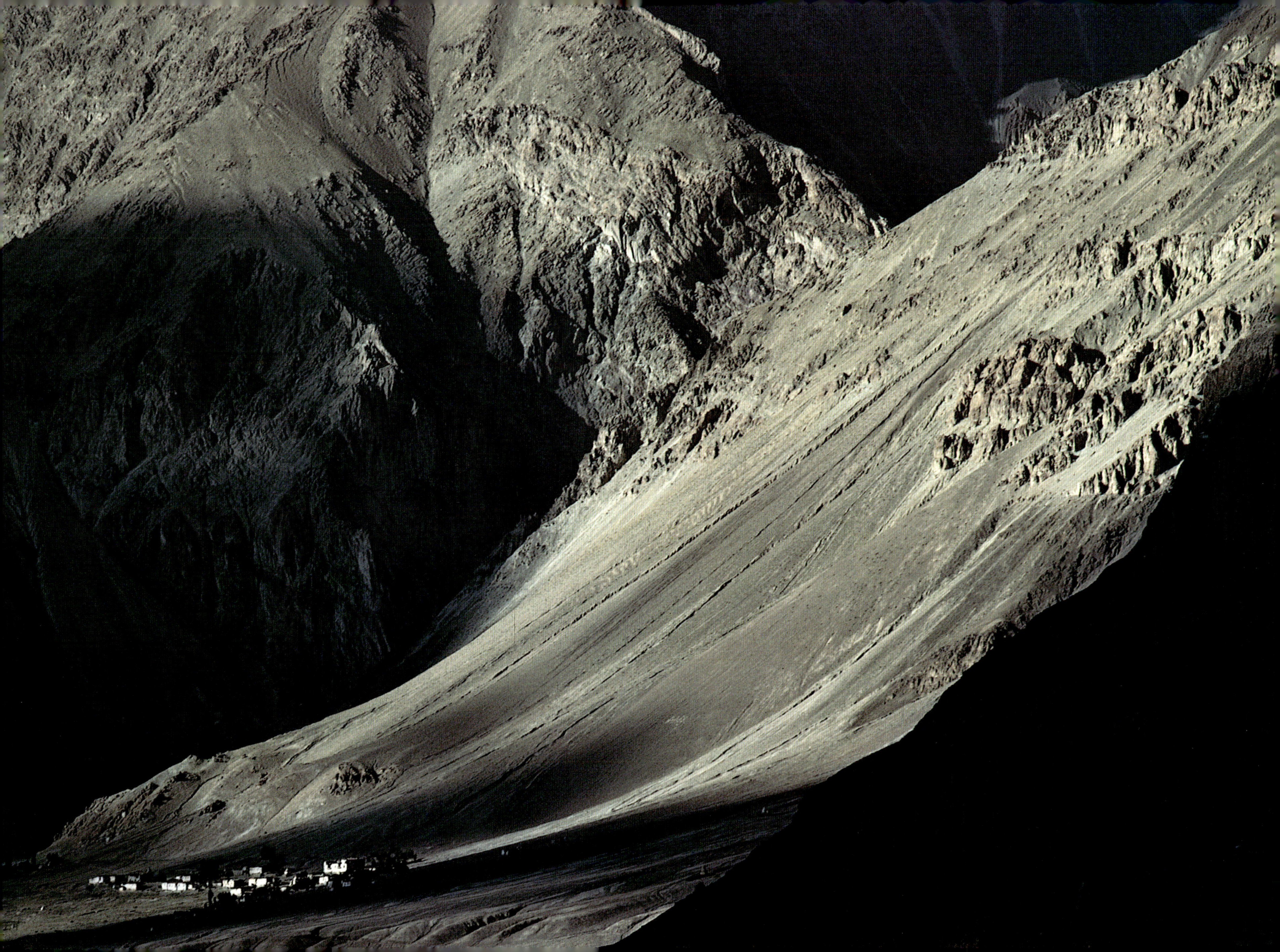

Almost completely blind now, her cheeks scored with wrinkles, Nawang Palden has forgotten how old she is. She lives alone; her husband and son were killed in the storm on the Shingu pass in the winter of the Year of the Dog.

In the autumn, her neighbour Dorjin comes and carries her on his back to the fields, where he sets her down on a wicker basket. And each day of the harvest she sits there beside the threshing floors in her long patched coat, gently waving her arms to chase away the sparrows.

In exchange for acting as a scarecrow, she receives grain, wool and wood from the other villagers. Nawang Palden beams with happiness. At the end of her life, she is still able to be useful.

She often prays, in the half-light of her kitchen with its earthen interior. When Daskit was born, I asked her to pray for a long life for the child. She calculated that she would have to pray for half a day if the gods were to hear her, and that it would cost me a fist-sized pat of butter.

While she was praying in a low voice, I left the butter and a ten-rupee note in the corner of the room. When I came back to see her, she thanked me for the paper which, she said, was such a good fire-lighter. She had torn up the note so that she would have some left for the winter when the days were damper.

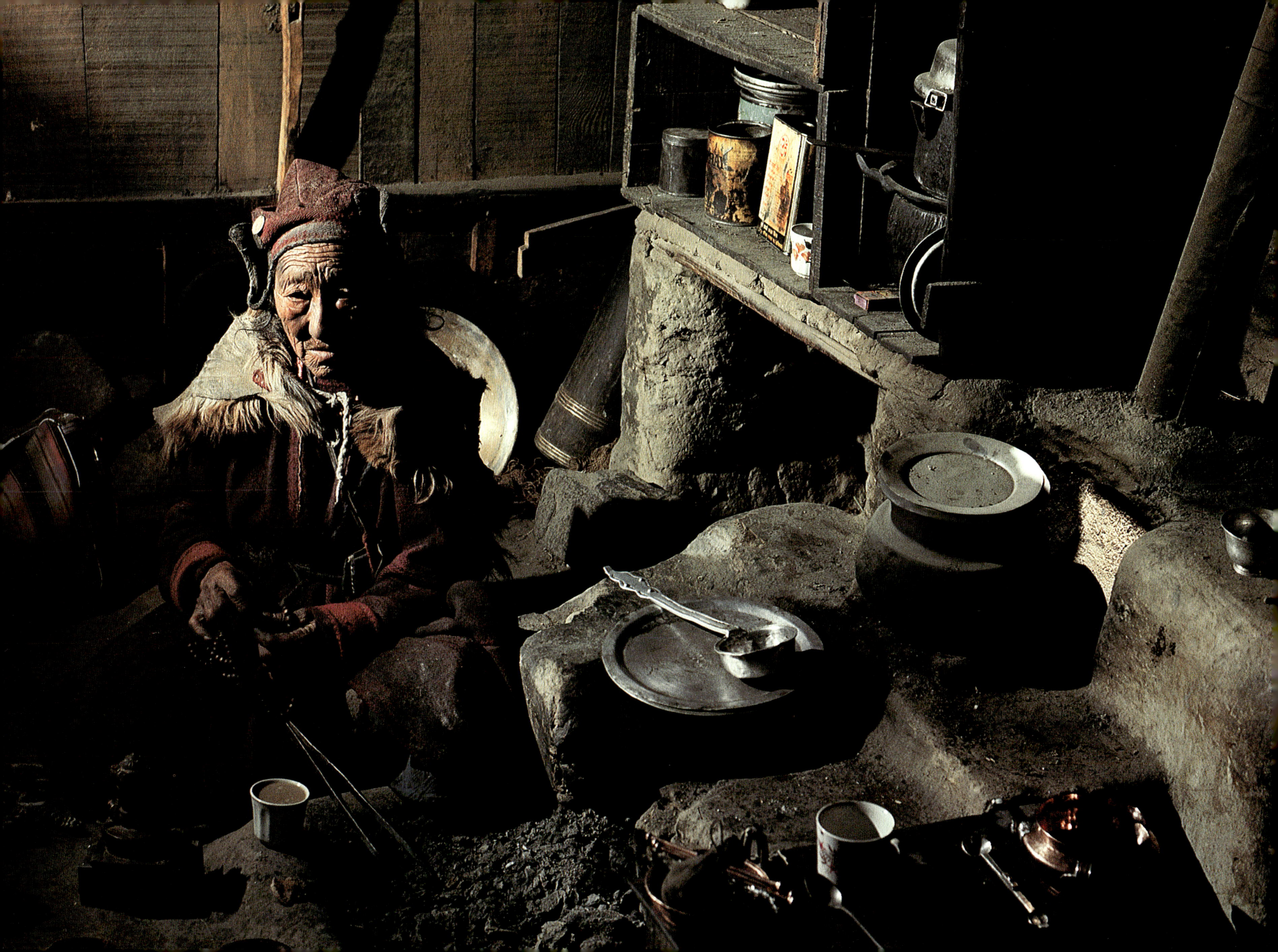

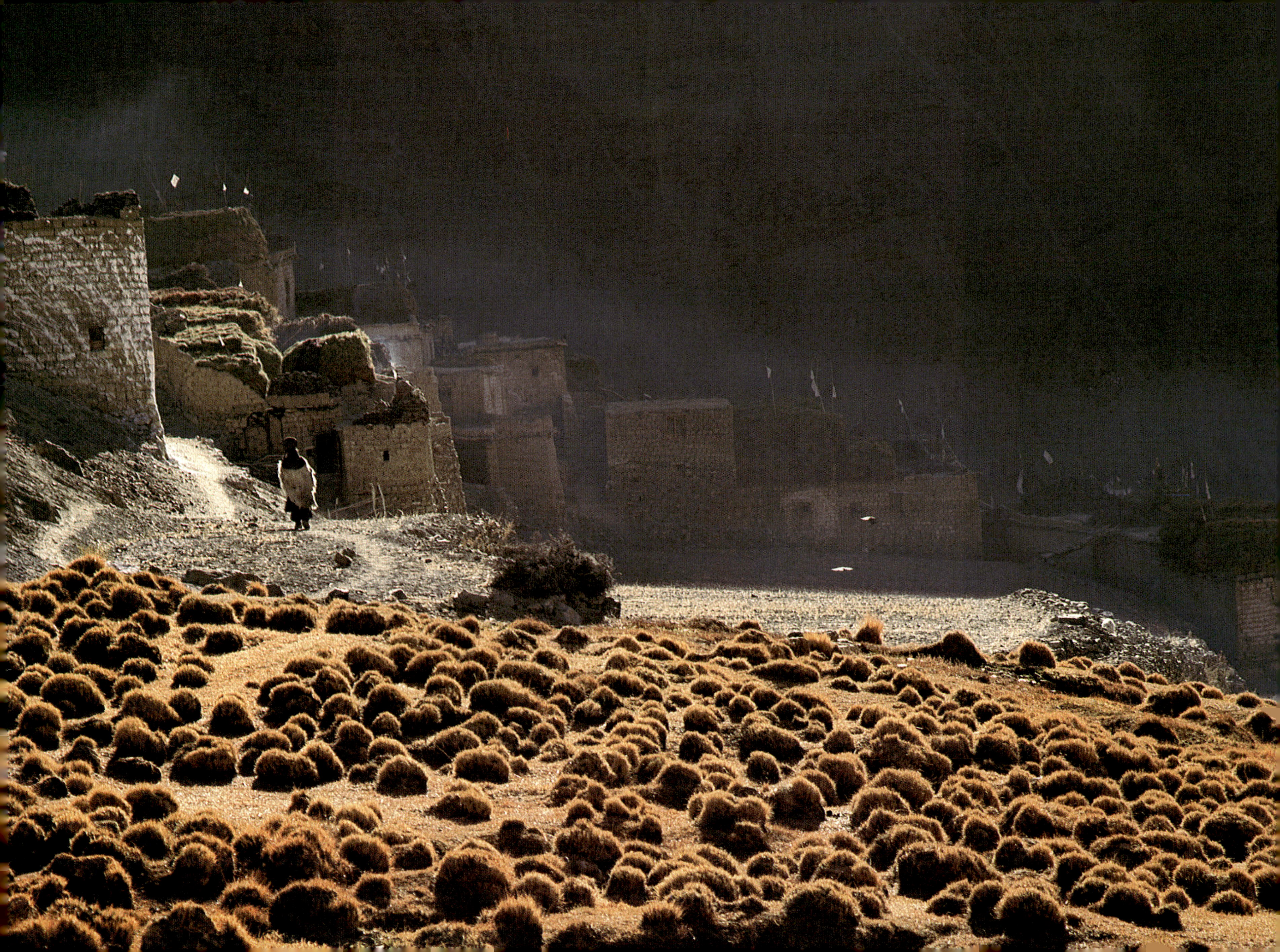

58

59

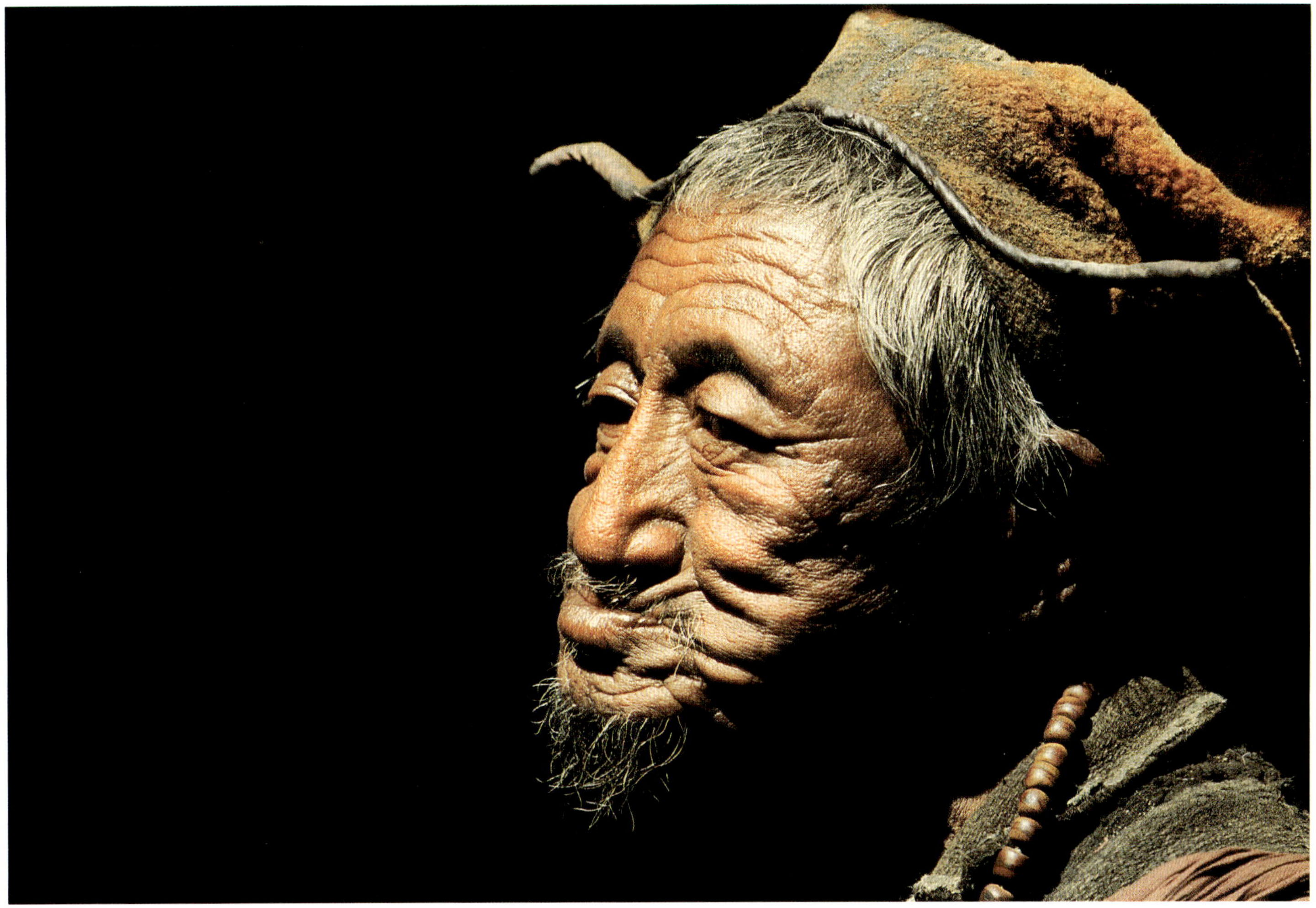

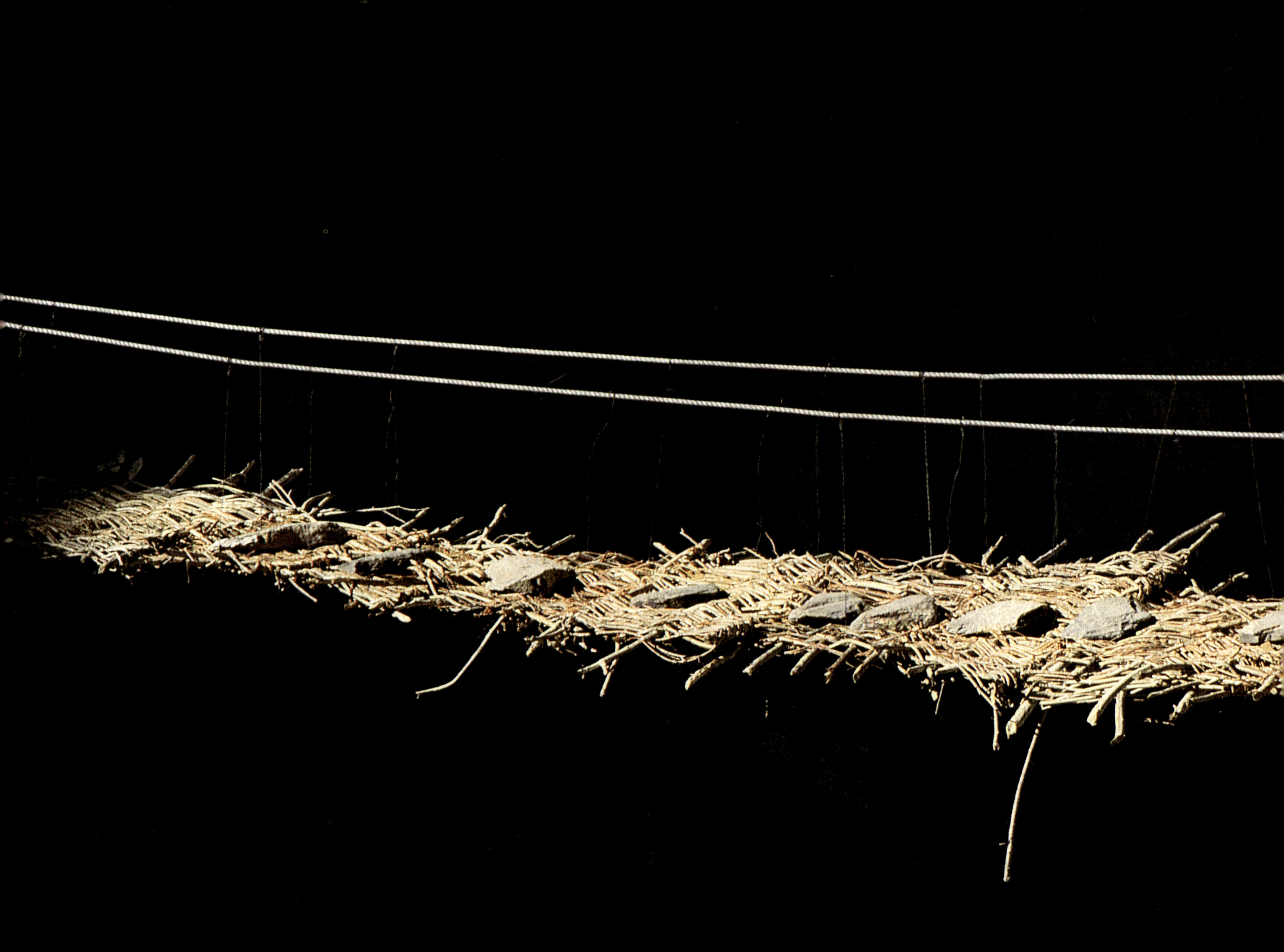

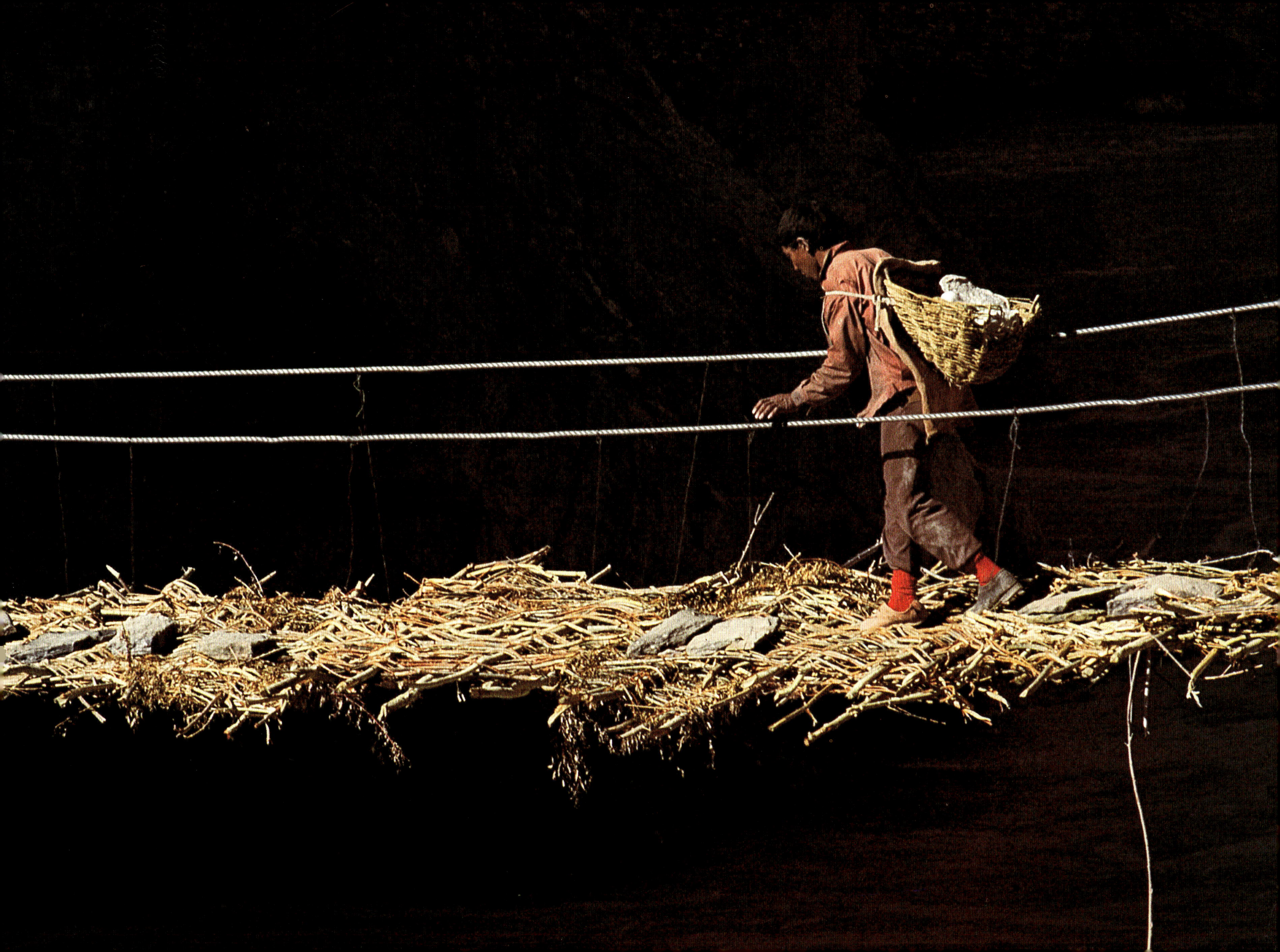

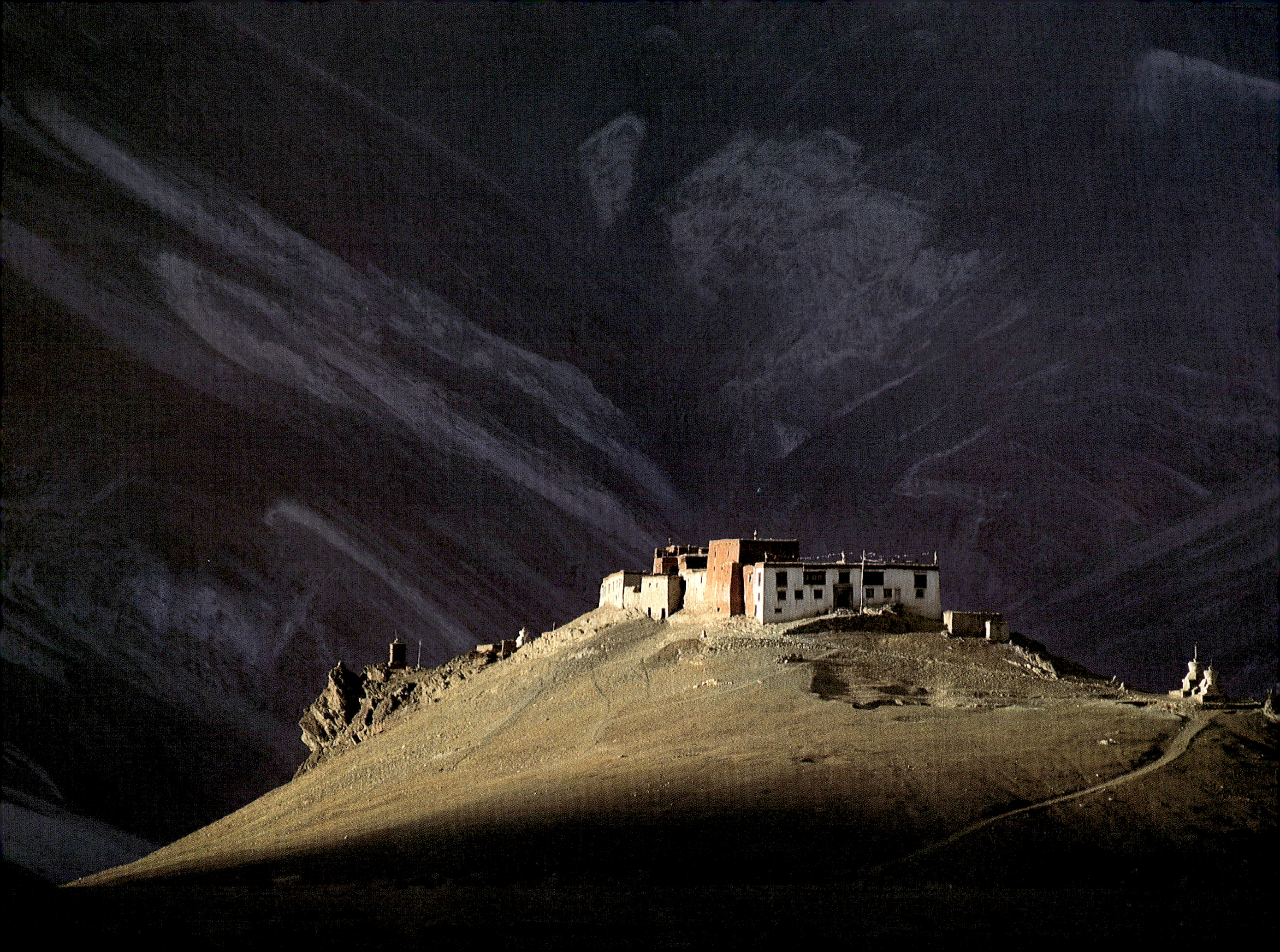

61 62

One night, when there was a full moon, Tsomo Yangkit came back late from the mill. On the outskirts of the village she saw a group of twelve people coming towards her; they wore no goatskins and carried no baskets. As she continued along the path, the figures in front of her became increasingly faint. Terrified, she hid behind a rock, clutching her amulet. The group faded into the darkness, leaving behind a single shadow which stood out against the moonlit slope. Strapped to its bare back hung a skeleton. After that, the spirit came every night to haunt her in her sleep. She would wake up drenched in sweat beneath her yak blanket. Then a monk recommended that, in order to confuse the spirits, she should change her name. So, from then on, she called herself Kusang Lamo, and the evil spirits never found her again.

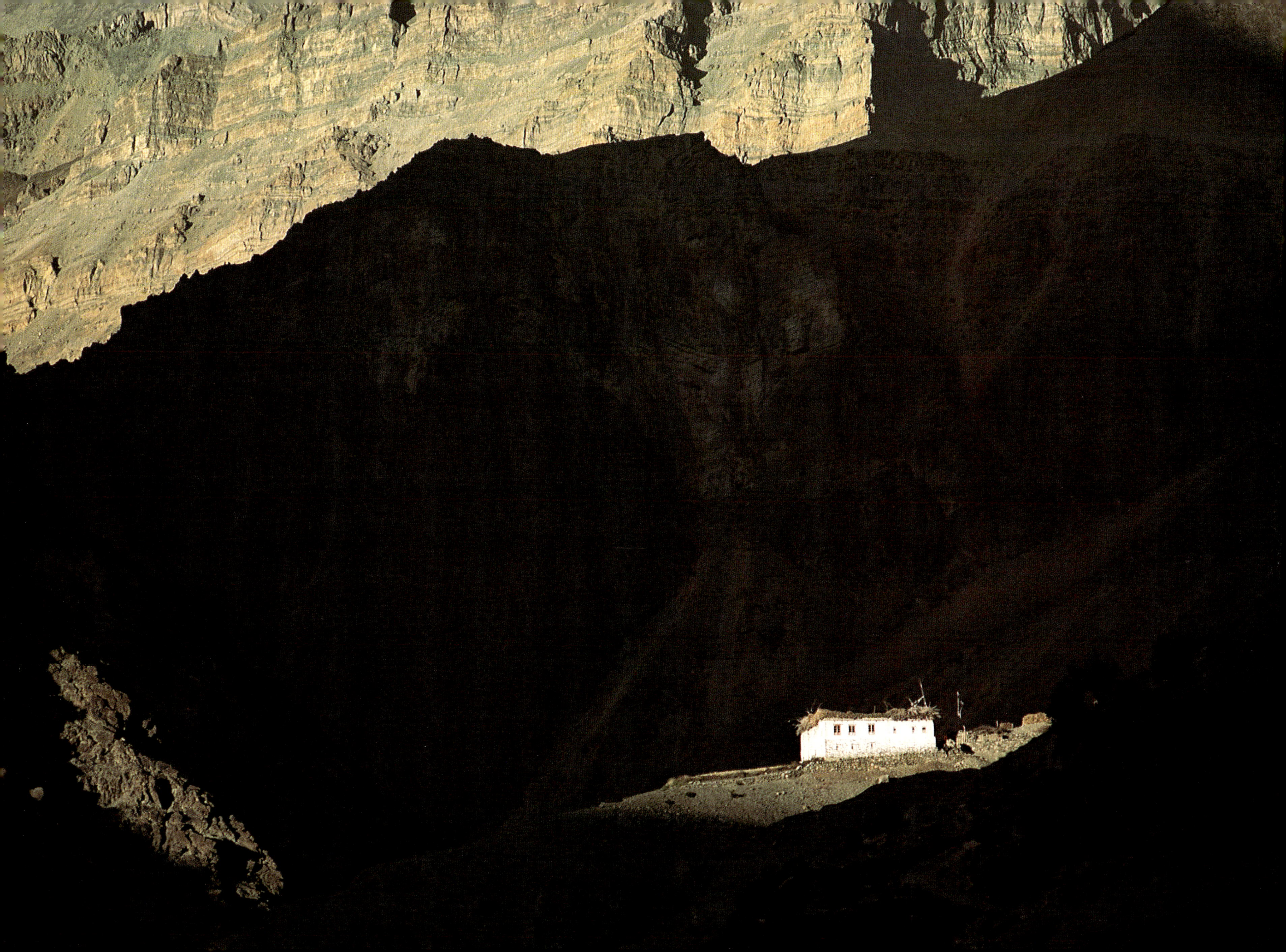

64

65

66

67

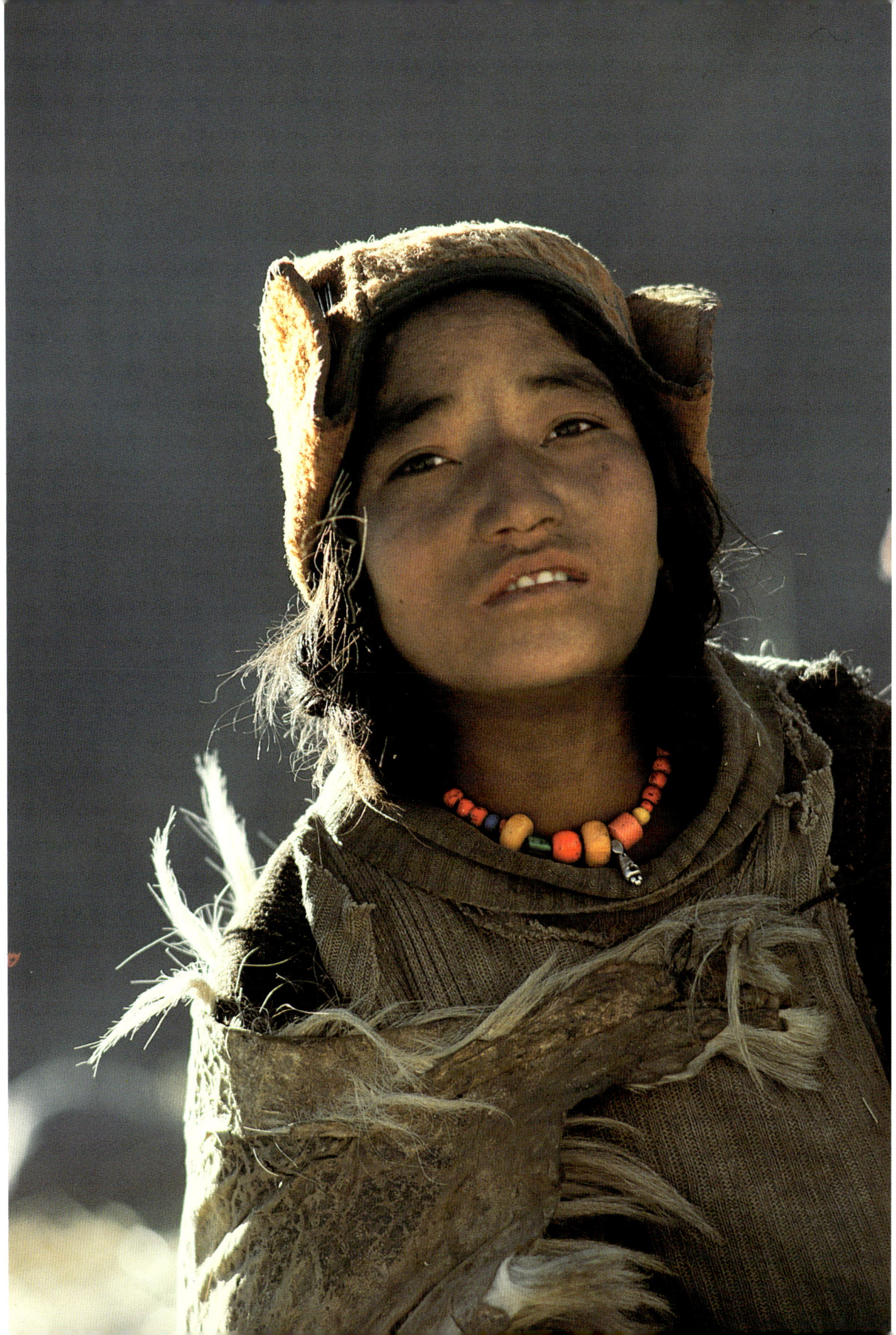

69

71

72

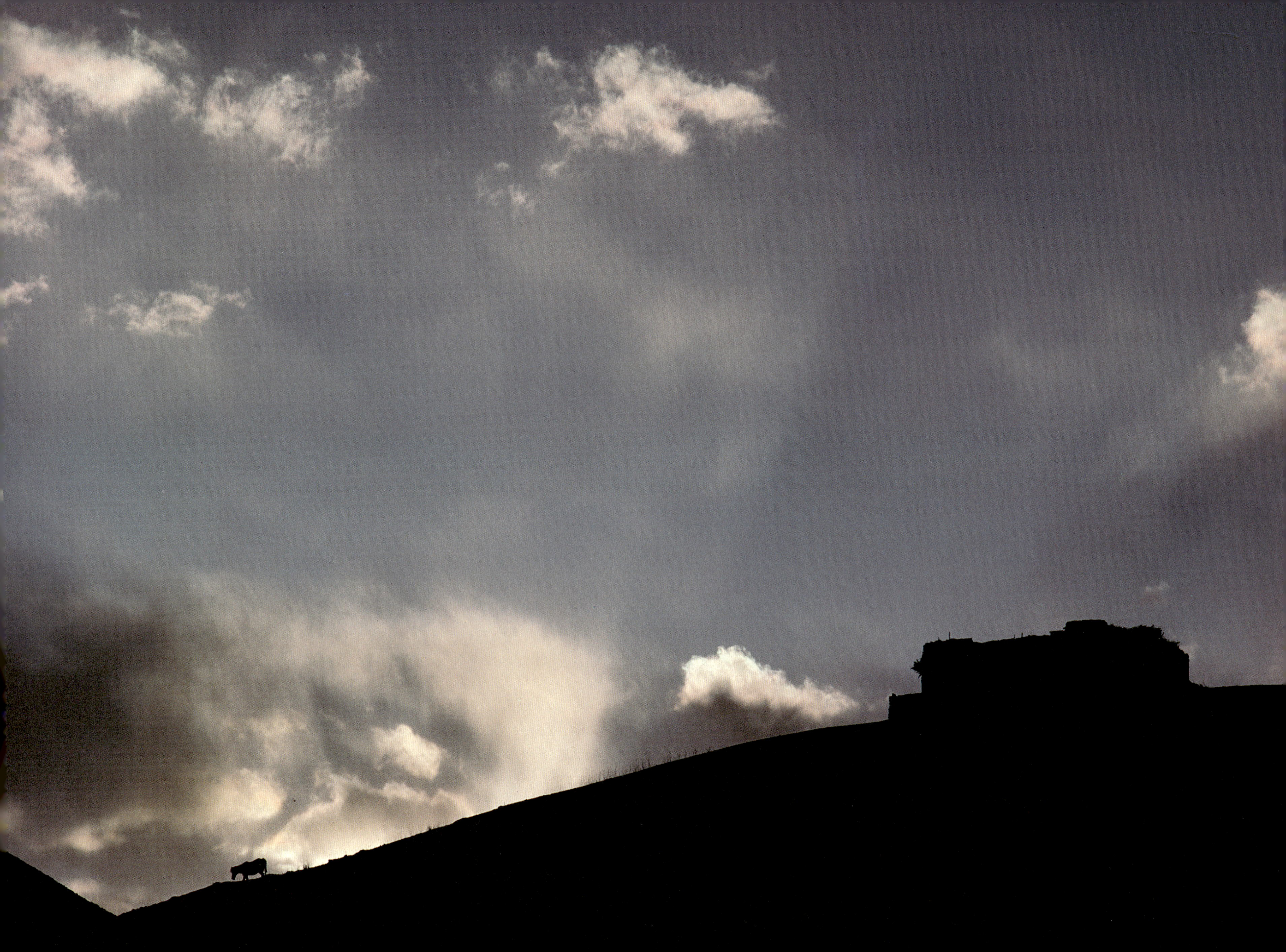

74

When daylight fades, the cosmic forces, the demons of the night, come to life. No one leaves the house then; the outside world belongs to the spirits of the kingdom of darkness. A dotted line guides the good spirits along the walls and into the interior of the house. But a demon snare, set at the entrance, traps the prowling maleficent spirit.

  'Evil spirits don't like chang', says Toyot. 'That's why you should drink a lot of it.'

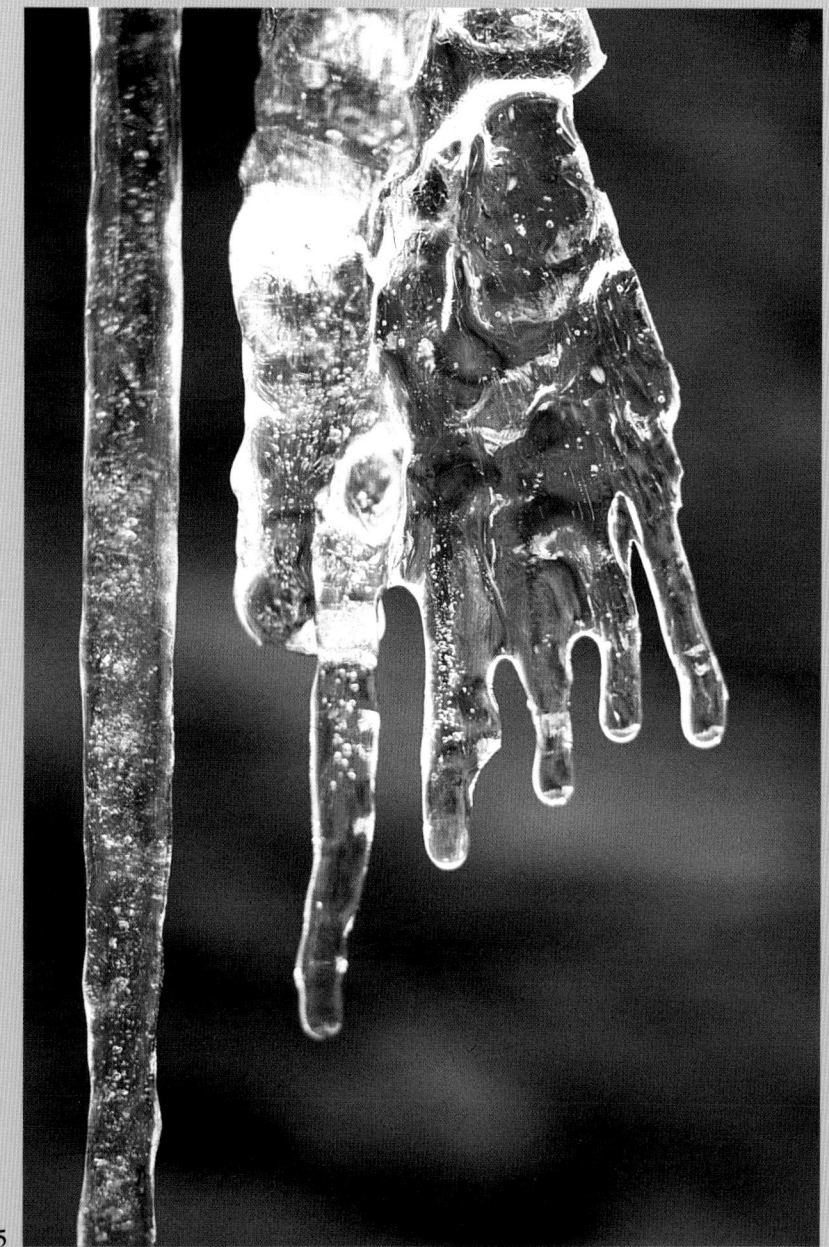

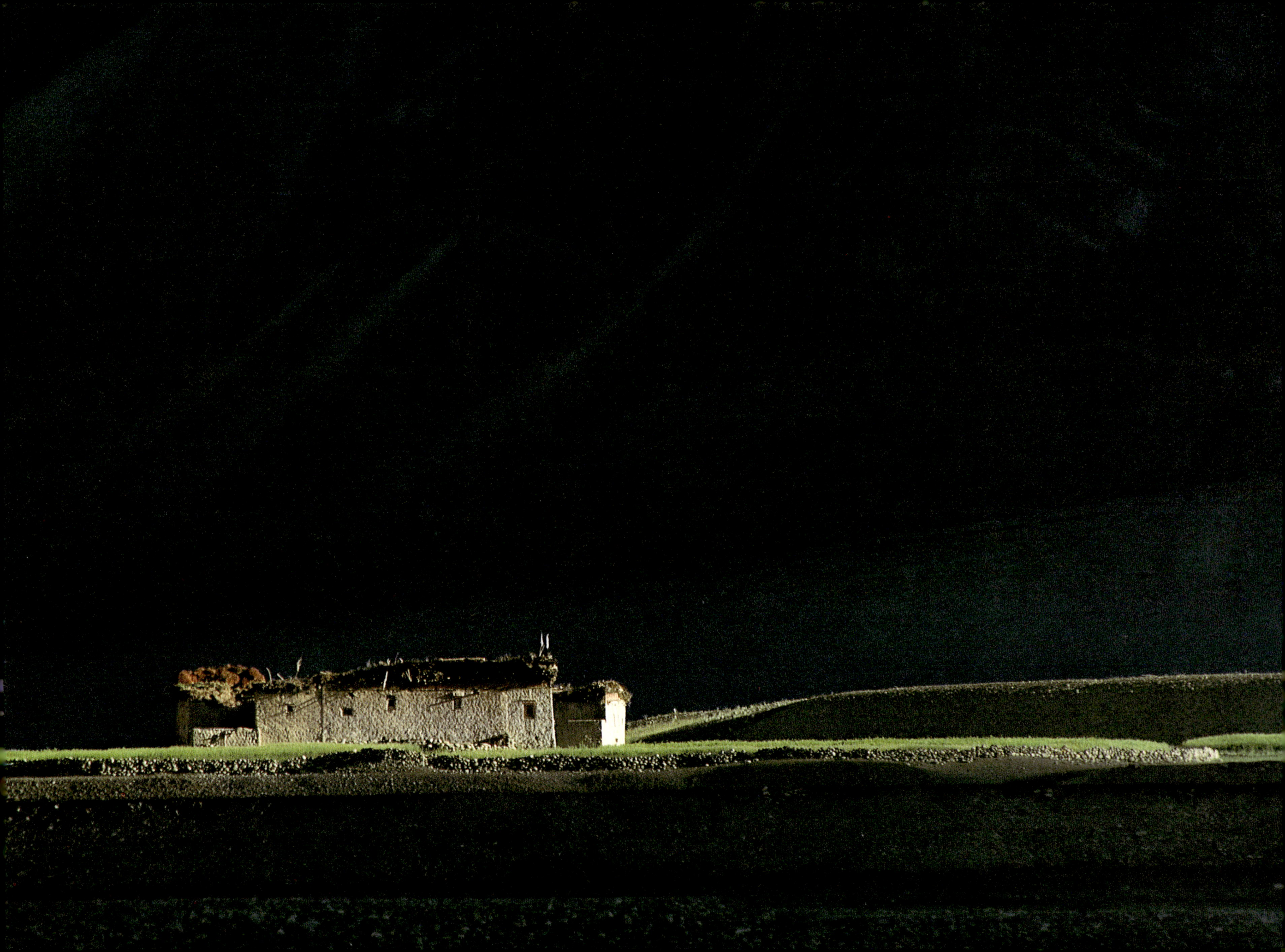

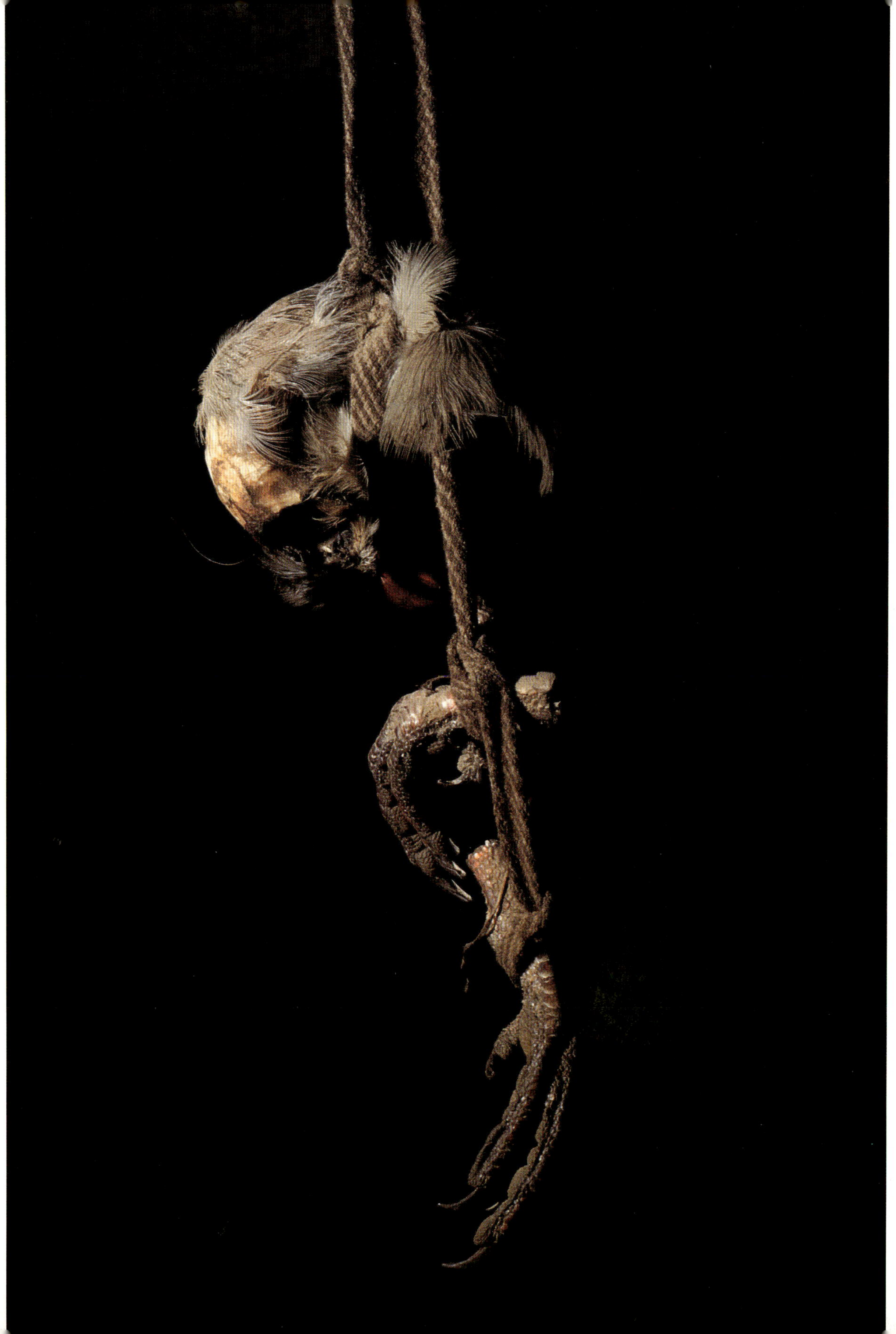

78

79

80

81

82 83

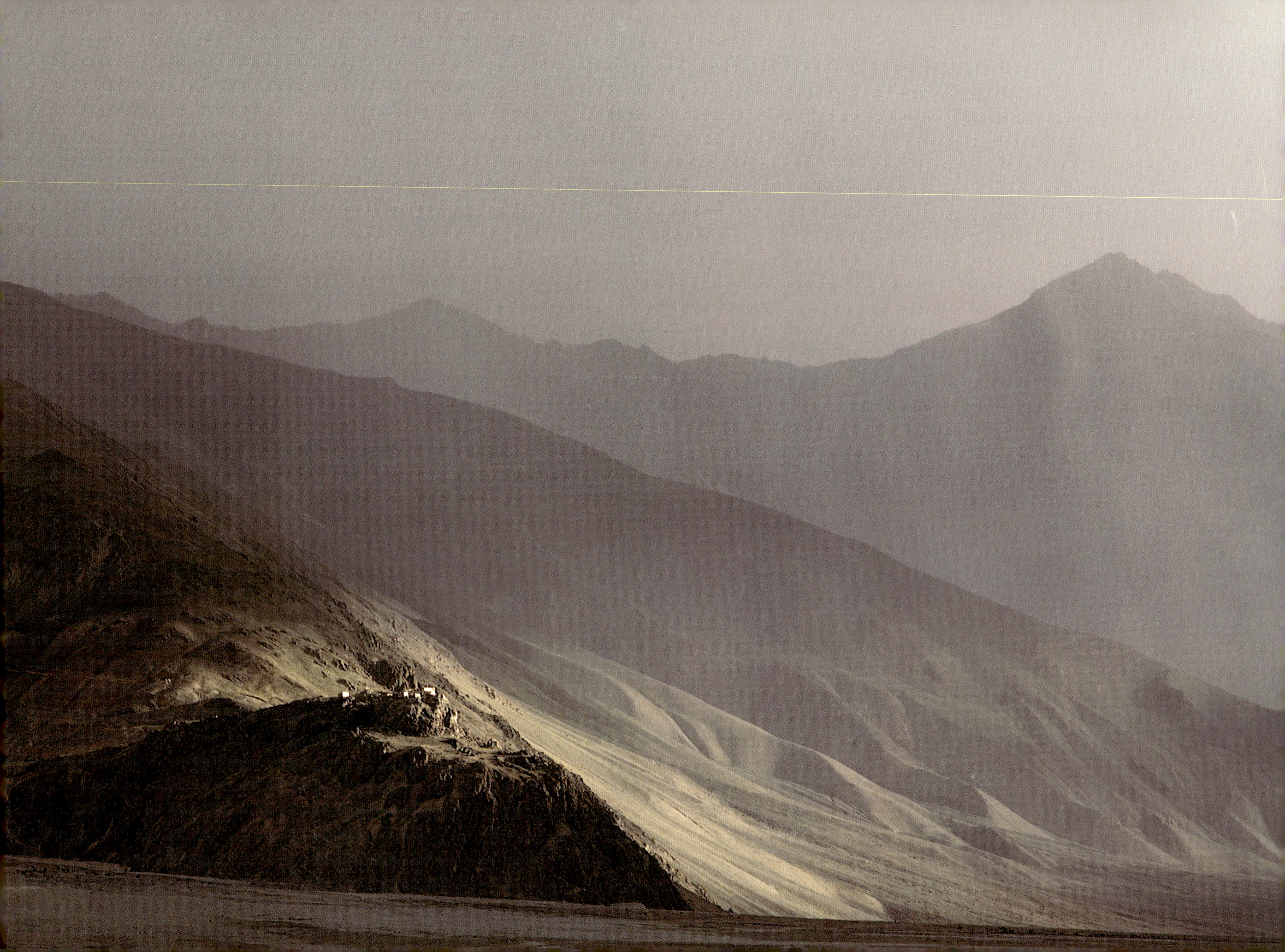

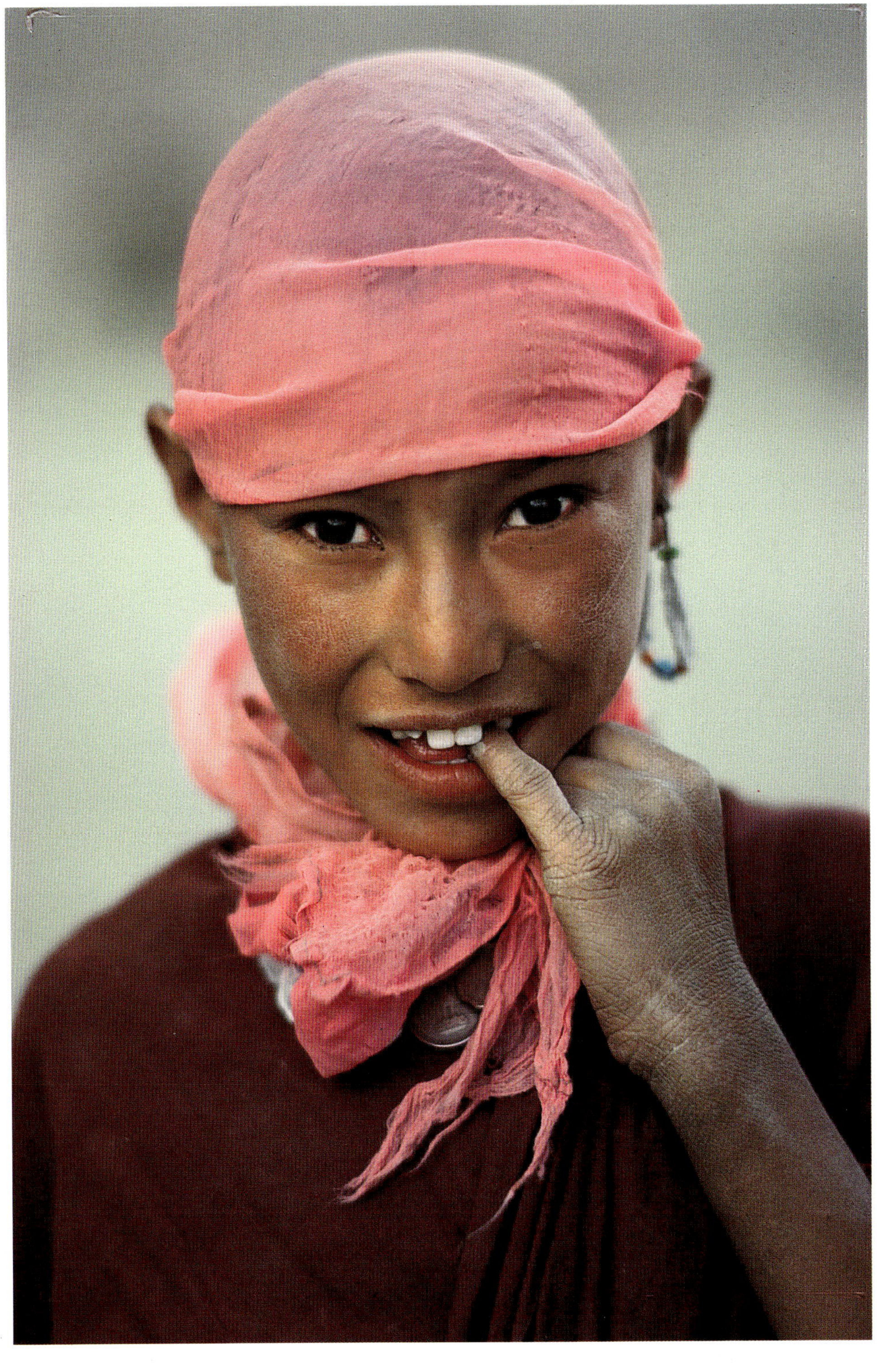

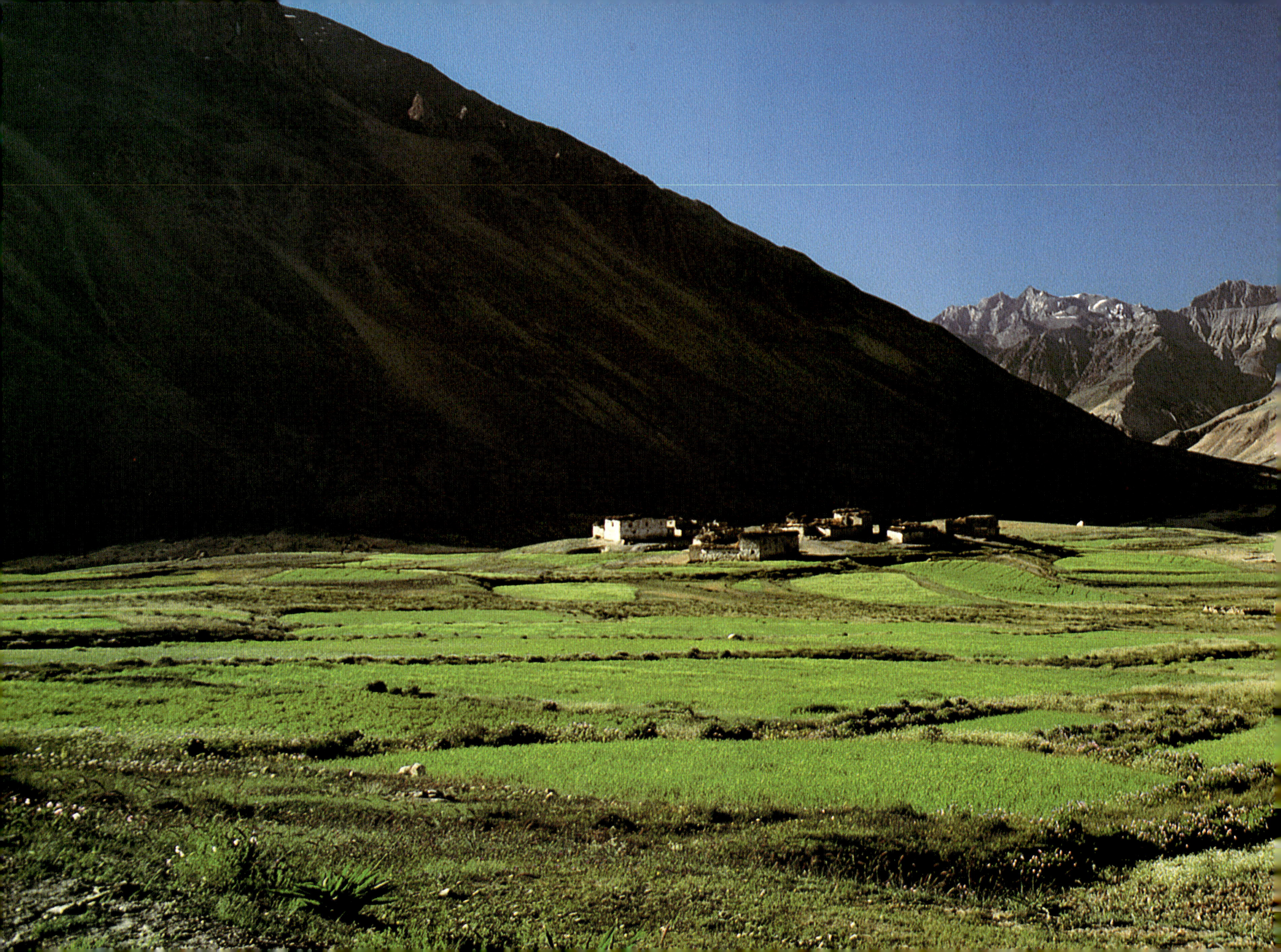

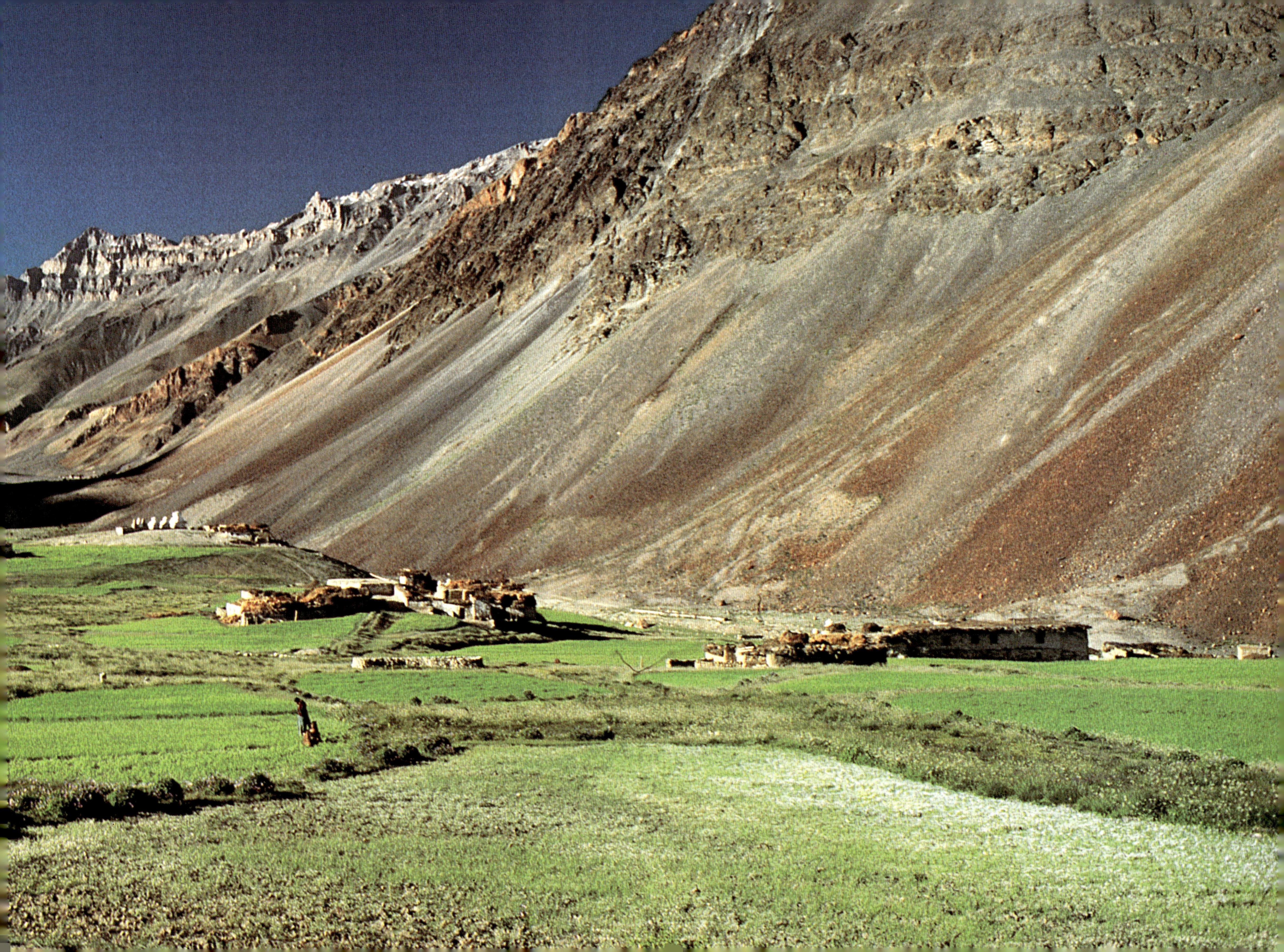

A month before he died, Tashi Namgyel Gyalpo, king of Padum, took me by the hand and said: 'We won't see each other again in this life. Don't be sad when you leave. I am content to die. I have achieved what I had to; now I shall continue my journey. Birth, being and change are in the nature of things. If we don't accept that our country, our culture and our existence have to evolve, there is no point in trying to understand the words of the Buddha. Study the teachings of those who are free, but be assured that true knowledge comes only with experience. You must live with your heart, on a level with other men, in order to discover the god that resides in each of us.'

88

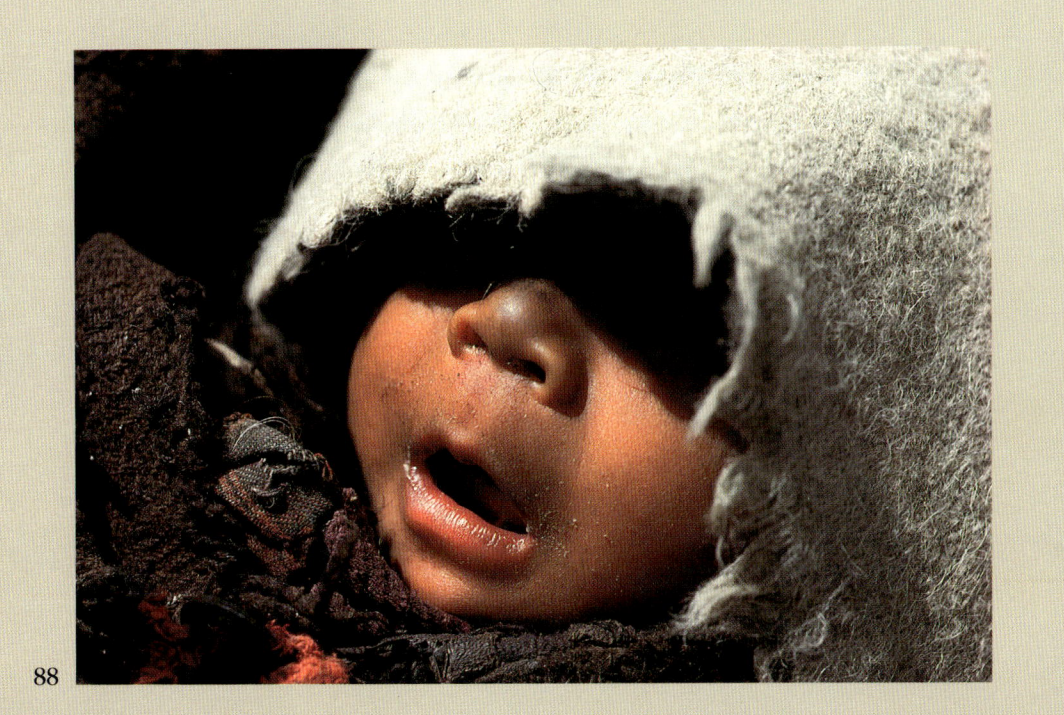

89

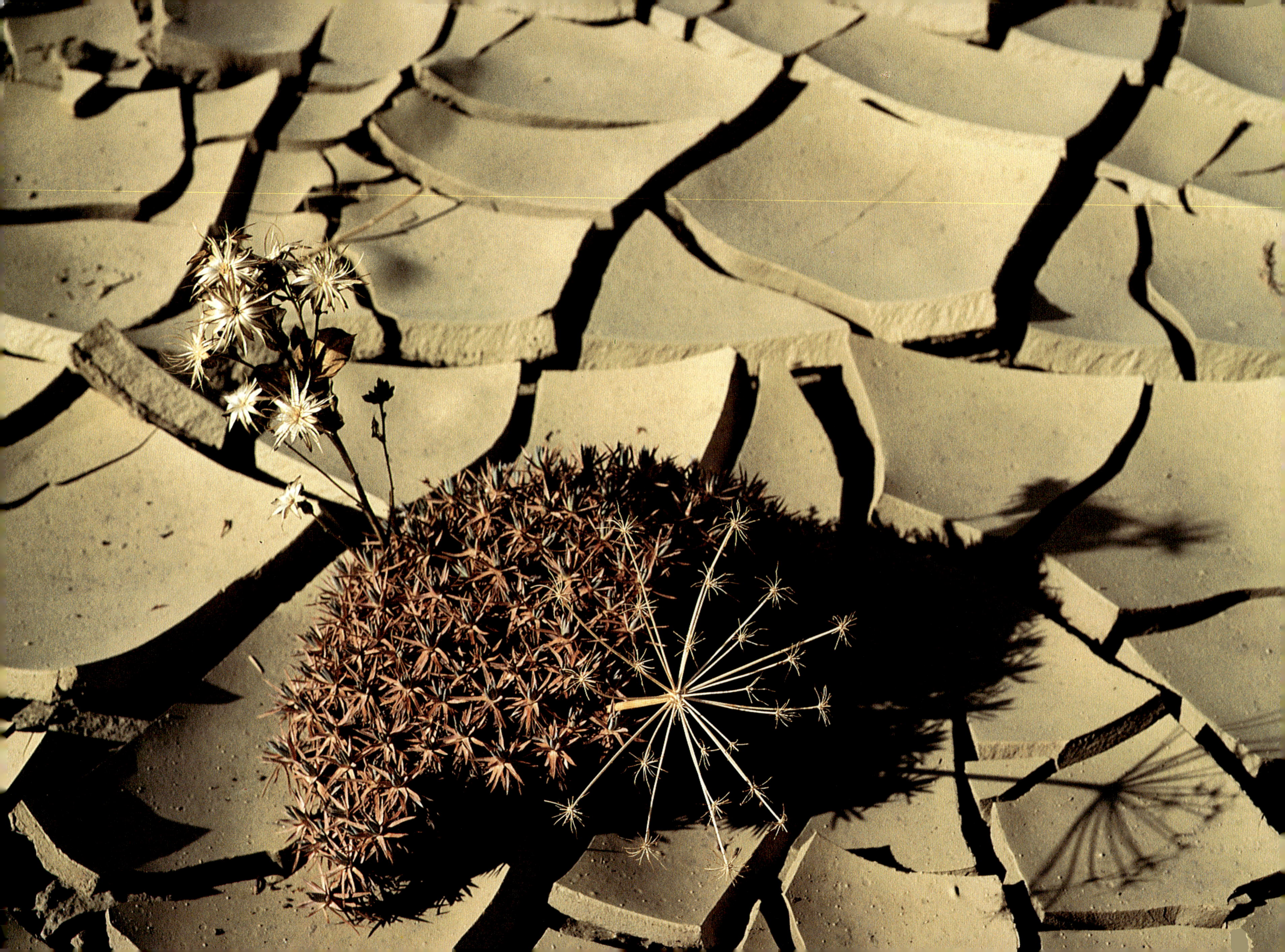

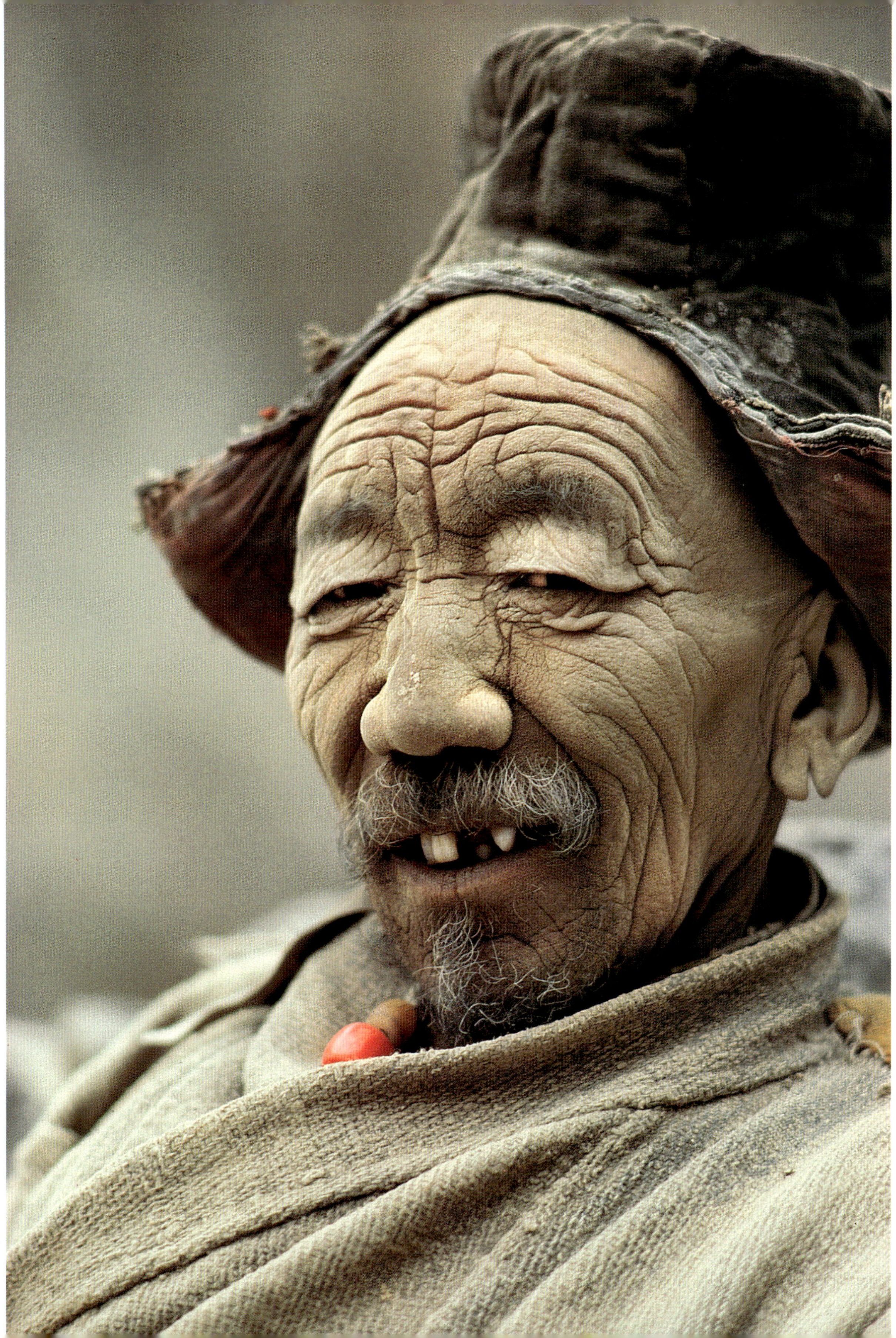

92

93

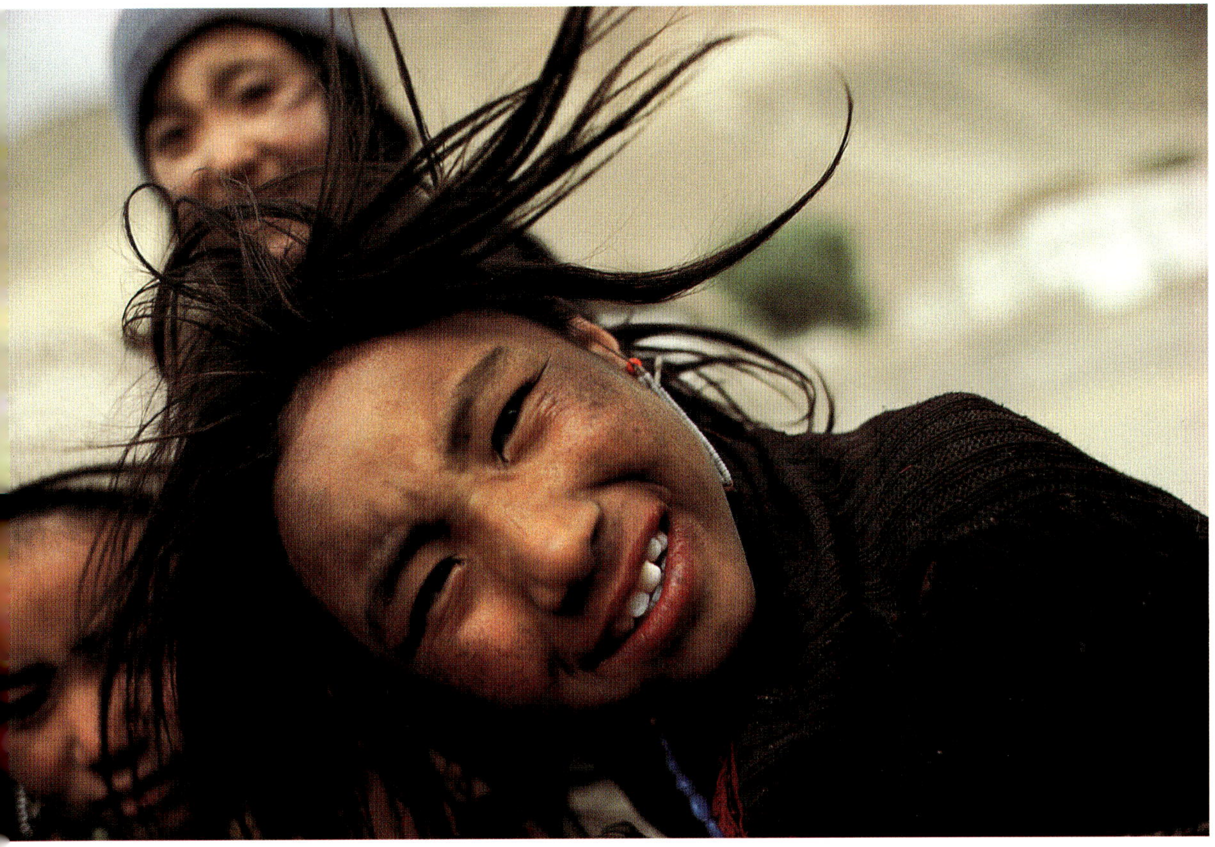

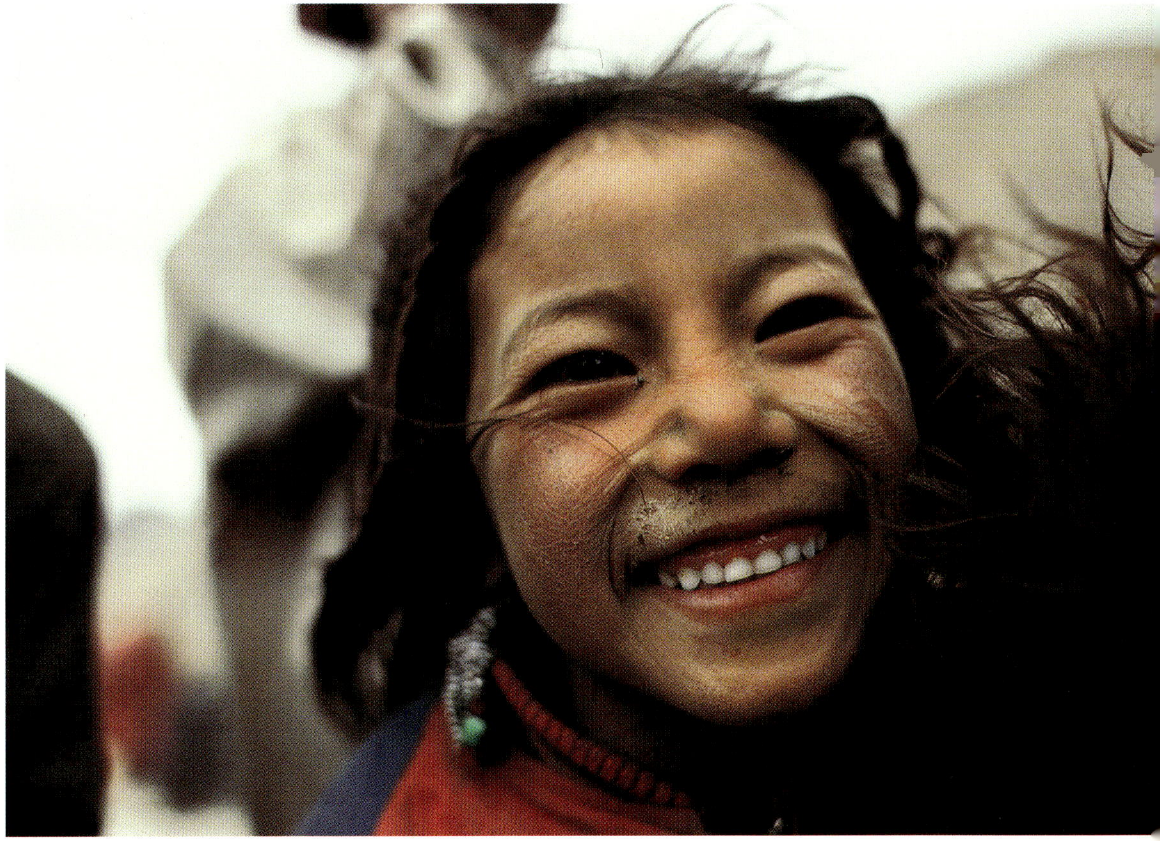

96 97

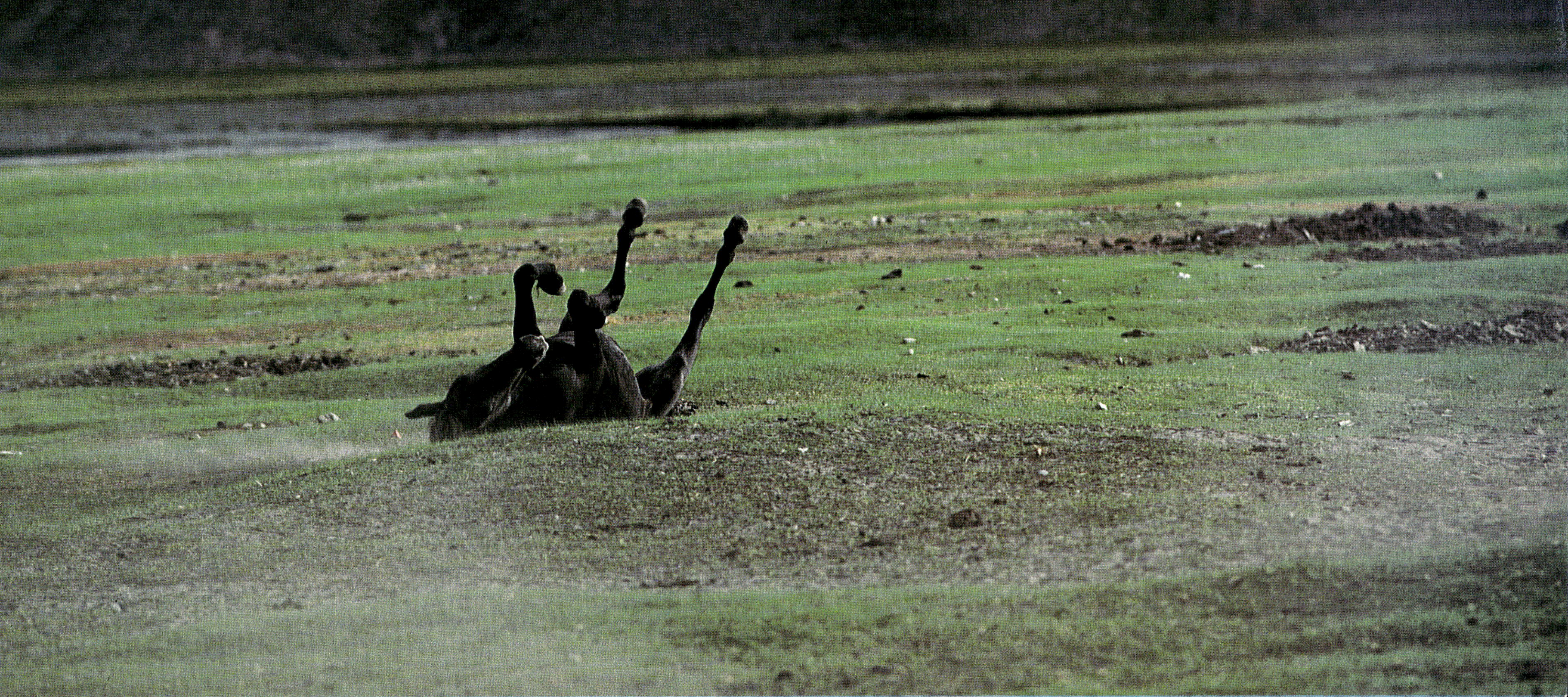

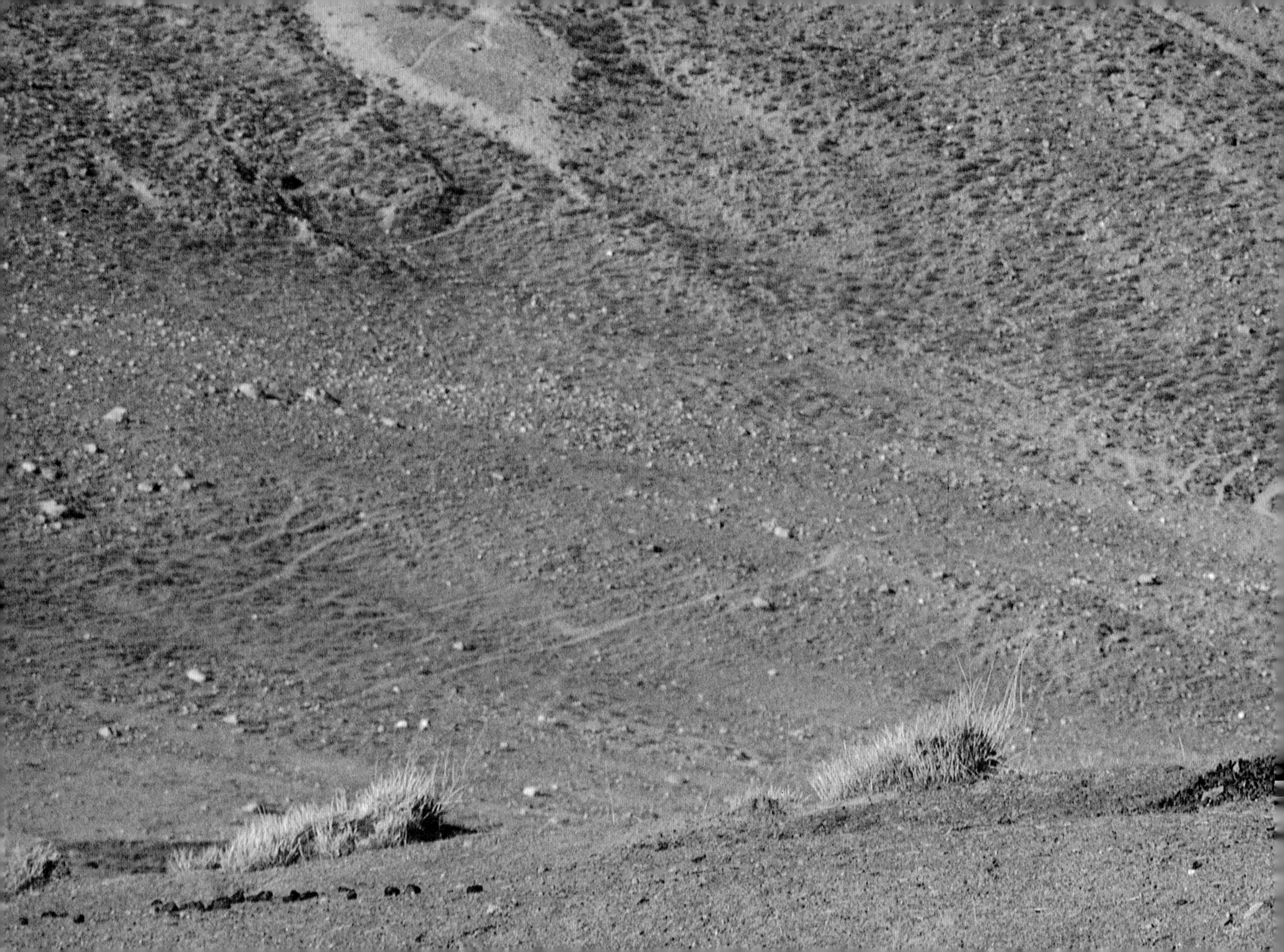

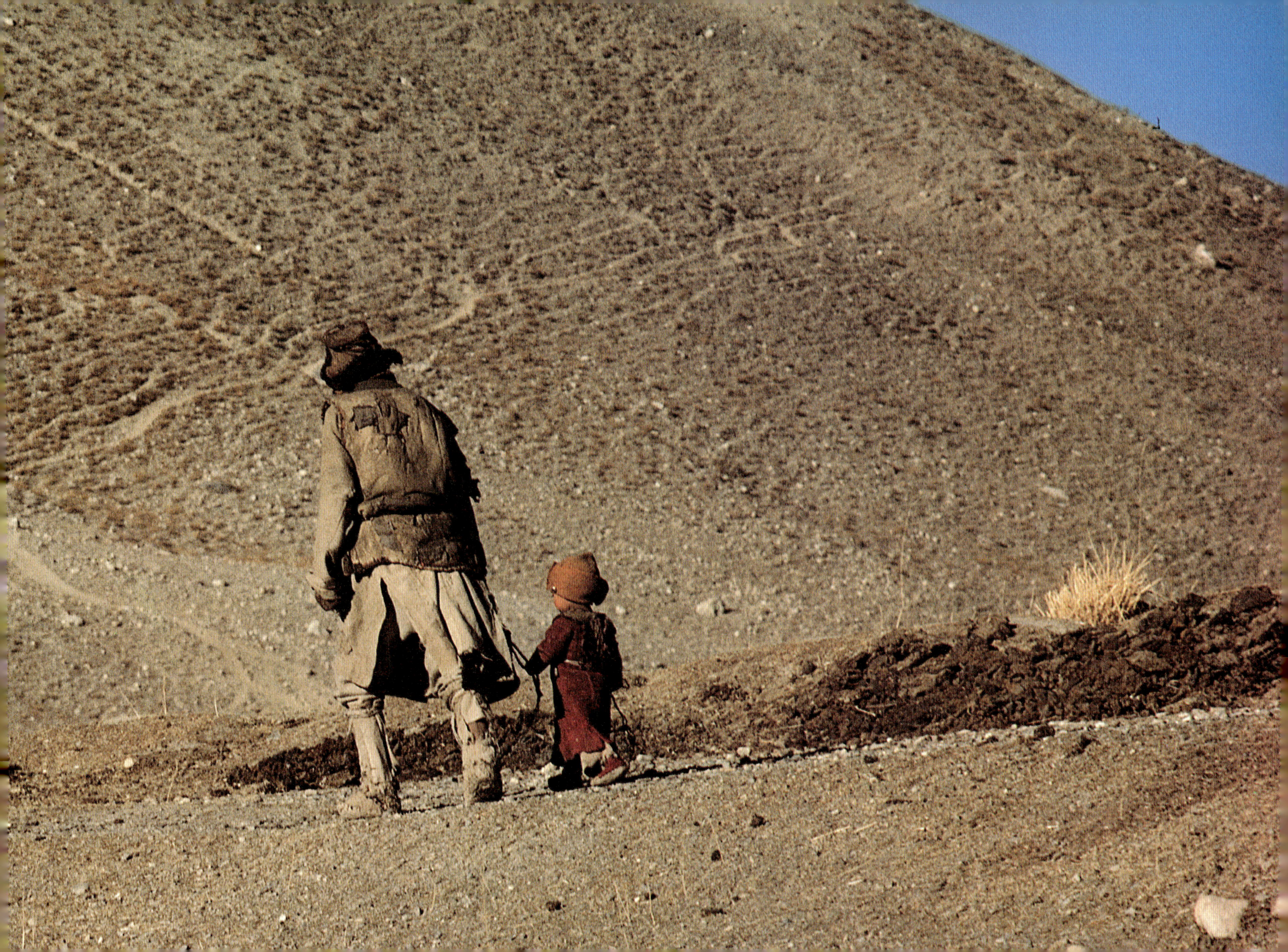

Little man, with your eyes the colour of sand, hazed with mist, wind and silence, if you only knew that this photo is no more than a pretext to get close to you...

99

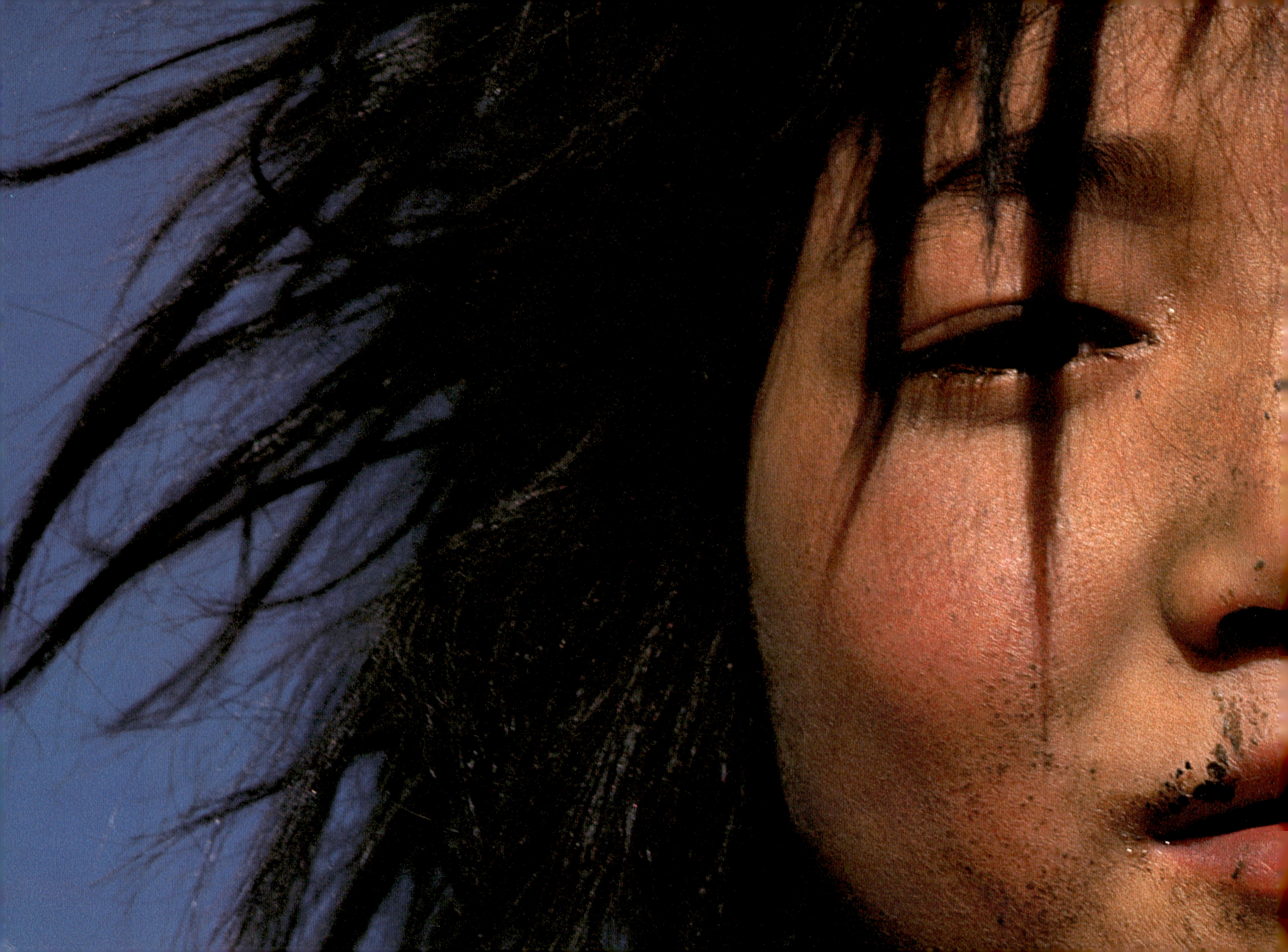

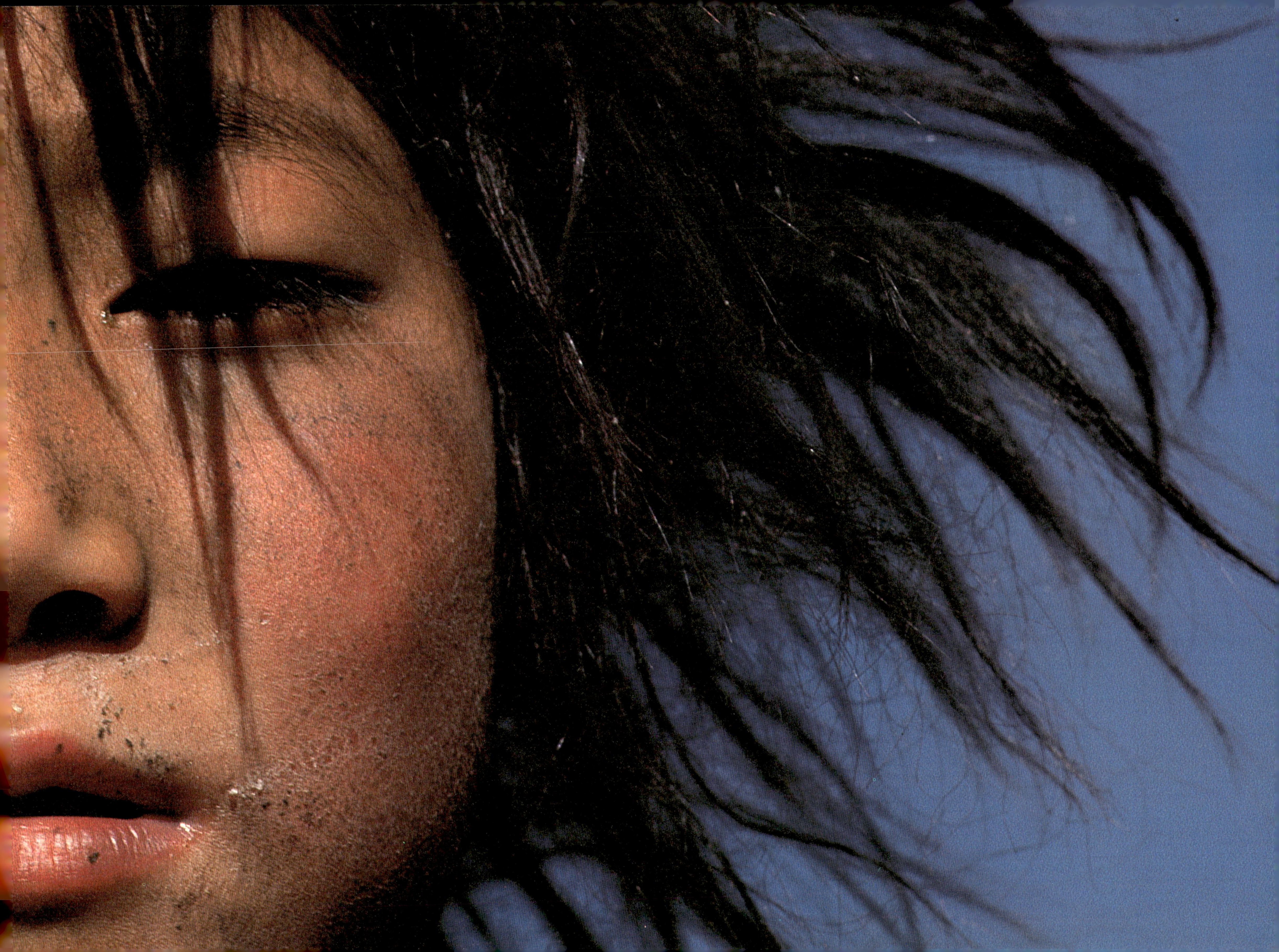

Captions

Endpapers: Stone engraved with the sacred words OM MANI PADME HUM (Respect the teachings of Buddha).

Title page: Shi. House flanked by seven *chörtens*, symbols of the five elements of life: water, earth, fire, air and space.

1. Group of women and girls at the *Gostor* festival in Karsha. Their headgear identifies their different status: *perak* (as in Plate 3) for married women; white 'balaclava' type for unmarried women; yellow or maroon cap for young girls or nuns.

2. Caravan on the plain, Padum. In the autumn the women climb the slopes of this mountain in search of bushes to use as fuel for their kitchen fires in the winter.

3. Testa. Wedding of Stenzing Dolma, aged sixteen. The young woman inherits her mother's *perak* and jewellery.

4. Village and monastery of Pipiting, at 11,500 ft.

5-6. The remote village of Shade (13,500 ft) in September, a five-day walk from Padum.

7. Rangdum Gompa. The three yaks in the far distance are going to Dibling, a two-day journey away.

8. Purni. Caravan on its way to the monastery of Phuctal.

9. Shalangtokpo ford, in the Shingu Pass.

10-11. Visit by a Rimpoche (reincarnated monk) to Shade. The young monks sweep the path as their master approaches on horseback.

12. Trangse, in July. The main house belongs to the married couple; the parents have moved into the smaller one.

13. Little boy in the fields. In summer the children wear very few clothes, so that they are not worn out by winter.

14-15. Zangla. The warm autumn winds raise clouds of dust. The child has been rubbing his eyes after a quarrel, and his face is streaked with dust and tears.

16. The village of Photaksar, on the road to Lamayuru and Ladakh.

17. Baby wrapped in a goat skin that has been turned inside out.

18-19. Each family has about ten goats, which are milked every evening.

20-21. The children rarely squabble. They acquire responsibilities at a very early age.

22. House in Yulsum, August. Four generations of one family live here.

23. The monastery of Karsha, which houses 150 monks.

24-27. The festival of *Gostor* at the monastery of Karsha. The monks' prayers are interspersed with dances performed by the newlyweds; the crowd watches and comments.

28-29. Monks and lay musicians at the *Gostor* festival in Karsha.

30. Whitewashed buildings housing the monks' cells in Karsha. The uppermost building, painted red, contains the chapels.

31. The monastery of Phuctal (13,000 ft), which houses fifty-two monks. The second son in every family traditionally becomes a monk. The monks live off the villagers' alms.

32. Wall painting representing one of the four guardians of the monastery.

33   The monastery of Phuctal. The main chapels are built within a cave.

34   Prayer flags, Rangdum Gompa. Each flag carries a prayer for the Buddha's compassion, entreating him to deliver the beings of this world from ignorance, passion and suffering.

35, 40   Frescoes at the monastery of Lingshed.

36   *Chörten* at the monastery of Phuctal, round which pilgrims pray.

37   Prayer at the monastery of Tongde.

38   Morning prayer on the terrace at the monastery of Phuctal.

39   An old monk at Tongde.

41   Fields at Tongde. Each family owns several plots of land; these are oval-shaped when they follow the contours of the mountains.

42-45   Typical poses adopted by Zanskari children.

46   September is the busiest month of the year, for it is then that the harvest and fodder – sufficient for nine months – have to be brought in.

47   View from the monastery of Tongde, 650 ft above the village. The snow-capped peaks reach around 21,300 ft.

48-49   September in Zangla. Animals trampling grain on the threshing floor.

50-53   Men and women take it in turns to toss the barley on to the threshing floor, singing and whistling for the wind to come and help separate the grain from the chaff.

54-55   The last of the harvest has to be rapidly gathered for milling before the streams freeze.

56   The village of Zangla, where one of the two kings of Zanskar lived until his death in April 1987. His palace dominates the village.

57   Padum's aged queen in her summer kitchen. Each house comprises a summer storey and a winter room, surrounded by the stables, on the ground floor.

58   The village of Shade in October.

59   An old man from Surle, aged sixty-six. The oldest inhabitant of Zanskar is over eighty, but average life expectancy is scarcely more than sixty. Half the children die in infancy.

60   Bridge leading to the monastery of Phuctal. Gradually bridges made of creepers are being replaced by cable bridges which the animals are able to cross.

61   The monastery of Rangdum, housing thirty-five monks. September.

62   Sacred texts from the Tibetan canon. The books are printed on long sheets of rice paper imported from Lahaul.

63   Kansar. A remote house in the valley leading to the monastery of Phuctal.

64-67   Zangla. Effect of sunlight and clouds during a September storm.

68   Seventeen-year-old girl, Kargyak.

69-70   First ray of sunlight gilding the topmost twigs of the trees at Shade and the slopes opposite the village.

71 Testa. First wisps of smoke of the morning as the barley soup is being prepared.

72 Surle. Young girls put on a bracelet made of shell or bone, which they will continue to wear for the rest of their lives.

73 Shi (13,500 ft). The animals return to the stable every evening. The villagers in the upper valleys make their main living from rearing livestock and exchange fodder for barley with the inhabitants of the lower valleys.

74 The yak is prized for its wool, its milk, its meat, its strength, its horns (used to preserve spices) and its tail (for use as a fly-whisk).

75 A block of ice frozen into the shape of a hand in the Jumlam gorges in September.

76 Evening sunshine at Rinam.

77 The head and feet of a chicken, placed at the entrance to a house, serve as a snare for frightening off evil spirits.

78-80 The houses are dark inside (light enters through a hole in the ceiling) and the rooms are always very smoky.

81 *Chang* is an alcoholic drink made from fermented barley and similar to cider. It is drunk at all occasions. To mark a particularly important event, distilled barley, known as *arak*, is served in a silver cup. Butter on the rim of the jug is a sign of hospitality.

82 The people of Zanskar are very religious. Everybody possesses a rosary with 108 beads.

83 In Zanskar it is generally believed that a rabbit lives on the moon.

84 October storm above the monastery of Tongde.

85 A girl from Rinam, whose father has brought her a shawl from Kashmir.

86 Shi at the end of July. Fields of barley, wheat and peas. In the upper valleys the fields are harvested at the last possible moment before the winter sets in, during the only two months of relative warmth.

87-89 New-born babies are frequently wrapped in a bag full of dried goat droppings which act as a nappy (or diaper).

90 Dried-up pond. Zanskar does not suffer real drought thanks to the melting of the perpetual snows.

91 A fifty-year-old man, covered in dust from repairing the track that leads to his village, Shade.

92-96 Tsazar and Zangla. The Zanskaris are a spontaneous people and love laughing.

97 Once free of the heavy loads which they have been carrying for hours, the horses like to have a roll.

98 Different generations live together under one roof. The family's survival depends on each person fulfilling his or her own role; each has a prescribed place in the family, and each is respected.

99-100 Olivier Föllmi caught unawares by his friend Serge Fouillet while photographing a little boy from Reru.

ॐ मणि पद्मे